The Mechanisms of Genetics

An Anthology of Current Thought

Edited by Stephanie Watson

The Rosen Publishing Group, Inc., New York

Published in 2006 by The Rosen Publishing Group, Inc.
29 East 21st Street, New York, NY 10010

Library of Congress Cataloging-in-Publication Data

The mechanisms of genetics : an anthology of current thought / edited by Stephanie Watson.
   p. cm. — (Contemporary discourse in the field of biology)
Includes bibliographical references and index.
ISBN 1-4042-0402-4 (lib. bdg.)
1. Human genetics—Juvenile literature.
I. Watson, Stephanie, 1969– II. Series.
QH437.5.M43 2006
599.93'5—dc22
                                                    2004024812

Manufactured in the United States of America

On the cover: Bottom right: A computer model of part of a molecule of deoxyribonucleic acid (DNA) shows the two strands of nucleotides twisted into a helical shape. Each strand contains an outer sugar-phosphate backbone (pictured here in yellow), from which purine and pyrimidine bases project (represented in blue and red). The four types of chemical bases link in complementary pairs, so that adenine links with thymine and cytosine links with guanine. Top: Digital cell. Far left: Digital cell. Bottom left: Austrian monk and botanist Gregor Johann Mendel (1822–1884).

CONTENTS

Introduction   **5**

1. Discovering Our Past Through DNA   **10**
"Living in the Past" by James Graff   11
"The Human Factor" by Nancy Shute   21
"True or False? Extinction Is Forever"
   by Luba Vangelova   27

**2. Mutation, Adaptation, and
   Natural Selection**   **32**
"Foresight in Genome Evolution" by Lynn
   Helena Caporale   33
"The Importance of Context in Genetics"
   by Frederik H. Nijhout   49

3. The Human Chromosome   **67**
"Why the Y Is So Weird" by Karin Jegalian
   and Bruce T. Lahn   68
"Centromeres" by Christine Mlot   80

**4. What Can Our DNA (and Animal DNA)
   Tell Us About Ourselves?**   **89**
"The Secret of Life" by Nancy Gibbs   90
"Metaphors and Dreams" by Tim Radford   97
"The Human Genome Project"
   by R. M. Gardiner   105
"Illuminating Behaviors" by Douglas Steinberg   119
"Bioinformatics—New Horizons, New Hopes"
   by Giridhar Rao   127

5. Genes and Disease   **139**

"Using SNP Analysis for a Clinical Look at Diseases"
    by Peter Gwynne   140
"Regenerative Medicine" by William A. Haseltine   147
"We Are What We Eat" *The Economist*   163

6. Modifying Nature with Genetics   **171**

"Food" by Jennifer Ackerman   172
"Improving Trout Through Genetics Research"
    by Sharon Durham   188

Web Sites   194
For Further Reading   195
Bibliography   196
Index   202

Introduction

Since the time of the ancient Greeks, men of science have pondered the biological and chemical interactions that make us distinctly human and that differentiate us from other species. But until the middle of the twentieth century, scientists knew very little about the inner workings of the human body and its functional unit, the cell. They had only a vague understanding of genes—the material that makes each person unique—and a similarly vague idea that perhaps genes were composed of a chemical called deoxyribonucleic acid (DNA).

But a pair of scientists—James Watson (1928–) and Francis Crick (1916–2004)—changed all that in the spring of 1953, when they announced that they had discovered the DNA double helix structure. The twisting ladder they described was composed on the two sides of sugar and phosphates, with steps made up of four chemical bases (adenine, guanine, cytosine, and thymine). The bases could unzip, allowing the double helix to replicate itself and pass along its genetic information.

Watson and Crick did not simply identify an obscure series of code within the DNA helix—they discovered the entire instructions for a human being. Their research, and the research of subsequent scientists in the field, revealed that the proteins for which DNA codes determine everything from an individual's height and hair color to his or her predisposition to certain diseases. For the first time, scientists could see the inner workings of heredity, and they could understand how genes are copied and passed from generation to generation.

At the time, Watson and Crick were seeking little more than knowledge of how proteins were made inside the cell. But as they celebrated their discovery at a pub in Cambridge, England, they must have had at least some sense of the historic implications of their discovery, as, according to Watson, Crick announced, "We have found the secret of life." Little did they know how prophetic those words would be. Within the century, their discovery would have monumental implications to scientists and citizens around the globe. It explained the mechanisms of heredity. It launched both the science of molecular biology and the multi-billion-dollar biotechnology industry. It enabled scientists to understand the genetic basis for disease, create tests to identify and even predict those diseases, and develop pioneer treatments that would have been unthinkable a half century ago.

Fifty years later, as the world celebrated the anniversary of Watson and Crick's finding, genetics had moved from a vague pursuit of a few enterprising scientists to a focal point of international research. In just a half century, scientists had learned not only what our genes look like and how they are copied and transferred through familial generations, but they had sequenced the entire human genome.

In April 2003, almost fifty years to the day after Watson and Crick announced the discovery of the DNA double helix, scientists from the International Human Genome Sequencing Consortium made a similarly momentous announcement. They had completed the Human Genome Project—the more than thirteen-year effort to sequence the entire 3 billion DNA base pairs in the human genome. They had mapped 99 percent of the gene-containing regions in the human body to 99.9 percent accuracy. And what they had discovered had shifted—sometimes radically—our understanding of the human genome. Before the project was launched, scientists had believed that humans had some 100,000 genes. Now they realize humans possess only about a quarter of the original estimate—some 25,000 genes. To the scientific community, completion of the Human Genome Project was the equivalent of man's first walk on the Moon.

Within the past few years, scientists have not only unraveled our genetic code but also mapped the genetic sequence of mice, yeasts, fruit flies, and nematode worms. What they have been able to discover about our similarities—and differences—has shed new light on the process of human evolution and illuminated the processes of disease.

Now that we have a working map of our genes, what can they tell us? They can tell us where we came from and give us a window into our future. They can show us how our ancestors evolved and where they migrated. They can help doctors predict which individuals are at risk for diseases such as Alzheimer's or cancer, then assist in the efforts to come up with more effective treatments, or even cures, for those diseases. They can identify treatments targeted specifically to the individual, treatments so specific to a person's DNA that they could one day reduce or even eliminate the incidence of harmful drug side effects.

Genes can also be used to design more nutritious and disease-resistant crops, and to create insects that spread a life-saving vaccine rather than life-threatening diseases such as malaria. Genes can be used to make animals more like us to provide organs for the thousands of people who now wait on transplant lists to get to the top of the list and to find a matching donor.

Although we have learned much about our genes over the last century, there is still so much more to know. Once scientists have sequenced all of the twenty-four human chromosomes and the more than 3 billion base pairs of DNA found in the human genome, they will have the instructions to a complete human being. But they will still need to learn how to read the instructions and decipher their meaning and how to use the instructions to improve the way we live.

The articles in this anthology chronicle the development of modern genetics and the breakthroughs that have transformed our understanding of the science that may one day reshape our lives. The authors included in this anthology (both scientists and science journalists) highlight significant points in the evolution of twentieth- and twenty-first-century genetic research—from Charles Darwin (1809–1882) and Gregor Mendel (1822–1884) to Watson and Crick and finally to the many scientists of the Human Genome Project. They reveal both the great simplicity and the incredible complexity of the human genome. And they show us just how far we've come in our understanding of the gene and how much more we still need to learn. —*SW*

1

Discovering Our Past Through DNA

Our DNA not only can help us learn more about ourselves in the present, but it also can provide us with a fascinating glimpse into our past. A relatively new research discipline—genetic anthropology—is merging well-established archaeological practices with cutting-edge genetic techniques to paint a clearer picture of who we are and from where we came.

Molecular anthropologists learn about our past and follow patterns of inheritance by comparing genetic material from modern humans with that of our ancestors. This article features two European teams of genetic anthropologists whose work has contributed to our understanding of our genetic roots. Ornella Semino and her colleagues at the University of Pavia in Italy followed the inheritance of the Y chromosome to trace the lineage of modern European men. In England, Martin Richards and his team followed the trail of mitochondrial DNA to learn how ancient migrations influenced our present genetic makeup. Because both the Y chromosome and DNA from the mitochondria (the part of the cell that produces energy) pass down from father and mother (respectively) virtually unchanged, these researchers have been able to get a clear picture of our genetic ancestry.

What both teams have learned from their research has challenged previously held theories of ancient migrations and has shed light on our differences from — and similarities to — our ancestors. —SW

"Living in the Past. Genetic Research Is Uncovering Signs That Our Ancestors Aren't What We Thought They Were—and That Most Europeans May Be Cousins"
by James Graff
Time International, April 30, 2001

As scientists clinked champagne glasses earlier this year over the formal publication of the human genome, there was a lot of speculation about how much this rough index to the secrets of human life would affect humankind's future, opening up new vistas for medical therapeutics even as it poses wrenching ethical dilemmas. But in order to look forward, we have to look back. The human genetic code is foremost a record of our quirky and adventurous past, scarred and spurred by accidental developments. All the evidence of our humble evolutionary beginnings is still there. Much of our genome is disturbingly reminiscent of that of the fruit fly, and 99 % of it all is shared with chimpanzees.

Somewhere amid what it says about our ancient past and possible future, our DNA conveys information about our more recent past—and perhaps the means to extend history into the realm of prehistory. And so it is that in the last decade, and at an increasing pace over the past few years, genetics has rejuvenated and somewhat confused the far older and dustier field of prehistoric archaeology. What had been a largely humanistic quest for first principles has been bolstered by complex statistical analyses of genetic evidence, allowing new voices to emerge from the long silence that makes up almost all of the history of Homo sapiens sapiens. In Europe alone, which manifests the least human genetic variation of any continent, genetic research is changing long-held notions of ethnic identity and origin. Among the most startling findings: some 80 % of the gene pool of modern Europeans stems from ancestors who came to the Continent more than 11,000 years ago. The vast majority of Europeans, be they Italians or Swedes, whether they pride themselves on their aristocratic or their peasant origins, can trace their ancestry to just seven female lineages and as few as 10 male ones. Most of them came to Europe as Paleolithic hunter-gatherers, and far from being wiped out by the superior technologies later brought from the Middle East by Neolithic farmers, they might well have lived side by side with the newcomers for millennia.

Alongside the classical archaeologists unburying, dating and correlating physical artifacts, a growing number of molecular anthropologists—or archaeogeneticists—are working to reconstruct the genetic heritage of modern Europeans. The data from the digs and the labs don't always sit easily with one another, and when increasingly bold ideas about linguistic ties are thrown into the mix, the discussion can get heated indeed. The tension among those disciplines is a creative one, though. "We have all different kinds of data, and a synthesis has just begun to emerge," says Colin Renfrew, director of the McDonald Institute for Archaeological Research at the University of Cambridge, whose own work has been spurring on that synthesis for decades. "But there's no doubt that in the end there was one past, where events happened in a place and at a time."

For the last few years, some of the most revealing remnants of that single past have been found not on archaeological sites, but in modern genes. Last year two separate groups of scholars presented evidence that modern Europeans are mostly descendants of people who came to the Continent in the Upper Paleolithic era, more than 11,000 years ago.

A group of researchers led by Ornella Semino of the University of Pavia and including Stanford University's Luca Cavalli-Sforza, one of the pioneers of genetic anthropology, analyzed data from the Y chromosomes of 1,007 men throughout Europe and the Middle East. Much of the gender-determining Y chromosome is passed on from father to son without recombining, but it is earmarked by certain telltale mutations. Semino's team found that just 10 mutations, each of which represents a lineage stretching back into prehistoric times, account for 95 % of all the samples taken.

By studying the way these mutations are distributed among present-day European men, and then comparing them with what archaeological sources have revealed about the Continent's settlement by humans, they concluded that 80 % of these chromosomes trace back to the most ancient migrations into Europe from Central Asia and the Middle East. These chromosomes had been carried by the people who survived Europe's last ice age in three refuges—one in present day Ukraine, another in the northern Balkans and a third in the Iberian Peninsula—before about 13,000 years ago, when they repopulated the vast regions of a Continent that teemed with large game as the ice sheets receded.

Those data meshed neatly with an analysis conducted by scholars at the University of Oxford of mitochondrial DNA, which is passed on exclusively from mother to child. Using more than 4,000 samples from current residents of Europe and the Middle East, Martin Richards (now of the University of Huddersfield) and his colleagues parsed out mutations that they believe originated in Europe. Using known mutation rates for a particular part of the mitochondrial DNA, they were able to distinguish the weight of subsequent migrations in the current genetic makeup of Europeans. Their strikingly similar conclusion: at least 80 % of the lineages of present-day Europeans stretch back to the Paleolithic era.

Those studies radically challenge previous theories of the ancestry of today's Europeans. The development of agriculture in the Middle East about 10,000 years ago is thought to have set off a veritable population explosion: archaeological sites have shown that the revolutionary innovation spread into the Eastern Mediterranean and the Balkans, then westward into Europe at a rate of about one kilometer a year.

The theory, fleshed out in detail by Cavalli-Sforza, was that a gradual but inexorable migration into Europe brought agriculture with it. Fortified by sheep, goats, barley and domesticated wheat, these Neolithic peoples were widely thought to have displaced the hunters and gatherers who had inhabited Europe—in much sparser numbers—until then.

The emerging genetic picture tells a different story, one that identifies the earliest Europeans as scraggly, persistent foragers who had hunkered down during the glacial age. "This research changes the whole debate about Europe, shifts it back in time from the Neolithic era of farming to the Paleolithic era of hunter-gatherers," says Bryan Sykes, professor of human genetics at the University of Oxford and a pioneer of mitochondrial DNA analysis. "There's now a much clearer sense that the genes we carry lived through the Ice Age, that our ancestors were hunting bison and reindeer with essentially the same genetic makeup we have today."

Like any other scientific innovation, tracing founder lineages through the Y chromosome of men or the mitochondrial DNA of women is open to many questions. Some scientists think, for instance, that even the relatively high number of samples—whether a lock of hair or a dollop of saliva—used in the most recent studies is still too small to give a full picture of genetic variation. Others harbor doubts that the rate of mutation of mitochondrial DNA is constant enough to support conclusions about chronological dating. "Physical anthropology remains the gold standard for dating," says geneticist Mark Stoneking of the Max Planck Institute for Evolutionary Anthropology in Leipzig, a member of the team at the University of California, Berkeley that in 1987 identified "Mitochondrial Eve" as the 140,000- to 280,000-year-old ancestor of all living humans. "But we're getting better at genetic dating all the time."

Carbon dating has been recalibrated in recent decades to give archaeologists strong certainties about the ages of key artifacts for Europe's prehistory, from the drawings in France's Chauvet Cave (32,000 years old), to possibly Neanderthal milk teeth found in Cavallo, Italy (31,000 years old), to the Minoan civilization on Crete (3,700 years old). That means there is always the prospect of a physical discovery—an agricultural site that doesn't fit in time or space, say—that can blow existing theories out of the water.

So, though anthropologists of even the most humanist bent can't afford to ignore the precipitous pace of discovery among geneticists, neither can any search for an integrated picture of the past rely on molecular anthropology alone. "Genetics tells us about the travels of human genes—the boy-meets-girl of the story," says Marek Zvelebil, an archaeologist at the University of Sheffield. "But gene exchange is different from language or cultural exchange. Who are we in the long term? There are at least three identities—genetic, linguistic and cultural—and we're all a mix of these."

Take for instance the key question of how agriculture spread in Europe. The genetic evidence of recent years certainly challenges the notion that agriculturalists from the Middle East wiped out previous immigrants to Europe, but it doesn't answer the question of how farming did spread. Zvelebil's reading of archaeological sites suggests that in many parts of Eastern and Northern Europe, there were porous frontiers between foragers and farmers that could last thousands of years.

In the Eastern Baltic, for instance, foragers traded seal fat, amber, slate and flint for the farmers' pottery and grain. In coastal regions where oysters or other shellfish were plentiful, foragers felt no particular compulsion to take up the tasks of horticulture. Where farming did spread, he says, it was often through a process of gradual adoption by hunter-gatherers rather than continual migration of farmers. "Gene flow just doesn't correspond to the cultural patterns," he says.

Nor, most scholars now agree, do they correspond very well to linguistics. Sykes has pointed out that the Basques, who speak a non-Indo-European language amid a sea of Indo-European ones, lack the genetic markers that would indicate they have been in Europe longer than their French and Spanish neighbors (though there are markers—such as a much higher frequency of RH-negative blood types—that point to their distinctiveness). And most speakers of Hungarian, a Finno-Ugric language surrounded by Indo-European tongues, don't appear genetically much different from their Slavic neighbors.

So what? Well, it complicates matters, suggesting that gradual cultural exchange has played a quiet but constant role in human history—and that invasions aren't necessarily all they have been cracked up to be. Thirty years ago the dominant theory was that the precursor of the Indo-European languages came to Europe on the tongues of warrior horsemen from the Pontic steppes of present-day Ukraine, and that the broad dispersal of those languages across the Continent was a tribute to their martial success. Then in 1987 Renfrew made a powerful case that it was the Neolithic farmers who brought the language with them from the Middle East, and that along with their barley and wheat they sowed the overwhelming domi-nance of their tongue throughout Europe. But as the genetic evidence now suggests, neither warriors nor farmers were able to keep their language to themselves. The Indo-European language family—from Lithuanian and Catalan to Swedish and English—spread far more successfully across Europe than the genes of its original progenitors did.

Linguists have their own ideas about how change occurs; they have managed through a rough philological equivalent of genetic research to work back from mod-ern languages to common roots, thus reconstructing Proto-Indo-European, a purely theoretical tongue.

But as Renfrew points out, if the difficulties of dating genetic change are vexing, the ones for dating linguistic change are even harder: though linguists can chart the rate of change from, say, late Latin to early Spanish, they can't prove the same rate applies for other languages before the advent of writing.

Renfrew sees evidence that linguists—like their colleagues in other disciplines when they look at prehistoric developments—are beginning to think outside the box and relate language to "tangible material processes" like floods, the spread of agriculture and demographic developments. Currently the prehistory of language is, as Renfrew puts it, "at the edge of knowability," but that could change in a matter of decades if the feverish pace of cross-fertilization of molecular anthropology and archaeology continues.

And there is no reason why it will not. "Thirty or 40 years ago the story of Europe was basically one of watching the covered wagons roll west, full of pottery, wheat and barley, pushing aside the hunter-gatherers," says Clive Gamble, an archaeologist at the University of Southampton. Further back, archaeology was harnessed to political ends, subsumed in Nazi Germany to the dogma of Aryan man, and in most other places in Europe to a kind of manifest destiny.

The new research is almost certain—like the genome itself—to suggest a more nuanced and complicated idea of what it means to be a human being. We are all more similar than racists or nationalists like to think: the genetic variance throughout the 6 billion humans on earth amounts to less than that in a single troop of chimpanzees. But those genes have afforded us an ability to adapt from foraging for hazelnuts to searching the Web in the evolutionary blink of an eye. What happens in the next blink is anybody's guess.

For decades, humans have pondered our relationship with our closest animal relatives, the apes. Pioneering evolutionary geneticist Svante Paabo has been studying the differences and similarities between human and ape DNA for more than a quarter of a century.

His work has been aided by a relatively new DNA analysis technology. In the early years of evolutionary anthropology, scientists had trouble isolating ancient DNA, often because it had been damaged over the course of thousands or even millions of years. But thanks to a technology called polymerase chain reaction (PCR), scientists can now analyze and replicate even tiny fragments of DNA, regardless of their age.

Since this article was published, Paabo and his colleagues have finished sequencing the chimpanzee genome. By comparing human and chimp genomes, he and his team have begun to discover why our two species are so different, despite our genetic similarities. Paabo

*and other scientists in his field hope that by
understanding what makes us different from
other species, they will learn even more about
what distinguishes us as humans.* —SW

"The Human Factor"
by Nancy Shute
U.S. News & World Report, **January 20, 2003**

LEIPZIG, GERMANY—Svante Paabo lopes through
the Leipzig Zoo, his long legs carrying him swiftly to
the new ape house. "These are the orangutans," he
says, reaching toward the glass to mirror the hand that
a shaggy orange ape has extended on the other side.
"They really like to go up to people. The gorillas ignore
humans; they can kill each other. And the bonobos
[pygmy chimps] have no violence, ever, and lots of sex."
This visit isn't just a walk in the park. The ape house is
also a laboratory, part of the Max Planck Institute for
Evolutionary Anthropology, which Paabo directs here
in the former East Germany. It's here to help answer a
question he's been chasing for the past 25 years: What
makes humans human?

For answers, Paabo, 47, is looking at DNA—from
humans, from a long-extinct human relative, and from
chimpanzees and gorillas like those at the zoo. He's
even sought clues in 2,000-year-old human feces from a
Texas cave. His finds have shed new light on how we
became so different from our closest ape relatives and
are offering tantalizing clues to great mysteries that
remain, such as the origin of language. "Svante is going

to be the first anthropologist to win a Nobel Prize," says Richard Klein, an archaeologist at Stanford University. "He just comes out with one paper after another that seems to be a breakthrough in human evolution."

Paabo first gained wide public notice in 1997, when he and Matthias Krings, a fellow researcher at the University of Munich, sequenced DNA from a 40,000-year-old piece of Neanderthal bone. The DNA was so different from that of modern Europeans that it quashed long-held theories that Neanderthals, the heavy-boned inhabitants of ice-age Europe, were our ancestors. Neanderthals apparently did not even interbreed with the humans who arrived in their territory 40,000 years ago.

Teamwork. That same year, Paabo got a chance to go after bigger questions when he was named director of the new Institute for Evolutionary Anthropology. It's an unusual effort, not only because it brings together DNA experts like Paabo with linguists, primatologists, and psychologists but also because of its lavish resources—a $9.4 million annual budget, $17 million for the ape center, and a $37 million new headquarters, set to open February 12. The cash comes as part of Germany's ongoing reunification efforts, but the interdisciplinary collaboration, many say, comes as a result of Svante Paabo.

As a boy growing up in Stockholm, Paabo dreamed of sailing south to explore the tombs of ancient Egypt. But when he started studying Egyptology at the University of Uppsala in the late 1970s, he was crushed to learn that it demanded not expeditions to the pyramids but memorizing hieroglyphic verb forms. "It wasn't cool." So he started studying medicine, his father's profession, and molecular virology.

Then he realized that Egyptian mummies and modern patients had something in common—DNA. Mummy DNA was cool. His old Egyptology professor helped him gather samples from museums. Working secretly, nights and weekends, he became the first to isolate ancient human DNA. In 1985, still a graduate student, he published a paper on his feat in nature and sent proofs to Allan Wilson, a pioneer in molecular genetics at the University of California-Berkeley. "I got this message: 'Dear Professor Paabo, can I come do a seminar in your lab?'" Paabo, floored, wrote back: "I'm not a professor, I'm not a doctor, I don't have a lab, but can I come to you?"

Wilson's lab was the first to show that DNA from living humans could be used to trace the origin of modern humans back to Africa. It was also one of the first in the world to use PCR, a chemical process that made it simple to copy DNA a billion times over, turning a mere trace into enough to study. Paabo had not been able to analyze the mummy genes, but with PCR, he believed, ancient DNA could open a direct window into the past—looking tens or even hundreds of thousands of years back.

With PCR, Paabo was able to duplicate DNA from extinct animals like the quagga, a type of zebra, and the moa, a flightless bird, swiftly answering long-standing questions about their relationship to living animals. Other extinct creatures followed, including mammoths, ground sloths, and cave bears. With Michael Hofreiter and other graduate students, he has also extracted DNA from the feces of ancient animals and humans, revealing much about their diet, behavior, and environment.

But in coaxing DNA from 40,000-year-old Neanderthal bones, Paabo may have pushed ancient DNA as far as it can go. Old DNA is hard to find; its nucleotides degrade when exposed to water, oxygen, and heat. "I've looked at something like 270 samples," says David Serre, a graduate student who spends long hours testing bits of Neanderthal bone cadged from museums and universities. "Only 20 of them still contain DNA." Worse, modern human DNA is on everything we touch. It can easily mislead researchers. Spectacular claims—such as one that Chinese researchers had extricated DNA from a dinosaur egg—were proved false when closer analysis revealed that the molecules were merely modern contamination. "It's rather embarrassing," Paabo says, rolling his eyes.

A relative. With ancient DNA giving just narrow glimpses into the past, Paabo is turning to what could grant a wide-angle view—the genes of the great apes. Chimpanzees, our closest cousins, share 98.7 percent of their DNA with humans. The trick is to find what in that 1.3 percent difference accounts for the things that make Homo sapiens special—language, reasoning, MTV. The chimp genome is being sequenced in labs around the world. When it's done, in 18 months or so, it should be a powerful tool for understanding how the species diverged.

For now, Paabo is fishing for another kind of difference. He is comparing patterns of gene activity in ape and human tissues to learn where genes are switched on and off. "We find so many differences, which is surprising," says Wolfgang Enard, a graduate student. "They are particularly pronounced in the human brain." The group has also found that methylation, a process that can adjust gene activity, is more prevalent in the human brain, suggesting it is a more finely tuned instrument. And last year, Enard found a key difference in the human and ape versions of Foxp2, a gene that was recently found to be essential for human speech. Mathematical analysis suggests that the human variation cropped up about 200,000 years ago, which could be about the time speech emerged.

To pin down the essential differences between the minds of apes and humans, the institute's researchers are also trying to identify what we have in common. Primatologists are studying culture—once thought to be exclusive to humans—among wild chimps in Africa. Psychologists are watching the baby chimps at the Leipzig Zoo and their drooling human counterparts in town. "For the first 10 months you can't tell the difference between chimps and humans," Paabo says. "Then the human children realize that behind your eyes is something that they can direct. That there are other people like me." Perhaps those children, too, will someday ask what makes a human human.

Cloning, or creating a living organism out of a cell from an adult of that organism, once seemed the stuff of science fiction. Then, in 1997, Ian Wilmut and his colleagues at the Roslin Institute in Scotland announced that they had cloned a sheep—the now-famous Dolly. Rather than arising out of the merger of egg and sperm, as humans and animals are normally created, the Scottish researchers created Dolly by placing the nucleus from an adult sheep cell into an unfertilized egg. That egg was then transferred into a female sheep, which carried it to term. Dolly, just like all clones, was an exact genetic replica of the cell nucleus donor.

Scientists have since cloned pigs, mice, cats, rabbits, and goats using similar technology. But Australian Museum director Mike Archer wants to take cloning one step further: he wants to resurrect the dead. He's not talking about creating a legion of flesh-eating zombies—nothing that horrific. Rather, Archer's team is trying to bring back the extinct Tasmanian tiger, or thylacine, using preserved DNA. The task is not an easy one. To clone an animal with living cells usually takes hundreds of attempts. And trying to pull viable and complete genetic material from long-dead cells is even more difficult. But the Australian researchers are hopeful that they can finish the task by 2010. —SW

"True or False? Extinction Is Forever"
by Luba Vangelova
Smithsonian, June 1, 2003

"DANGER," says the sign on the door of a laboratory at the Australian Museum in Sydney: "Tasmanian Tiger, Trespassers will be eaten!" The joke is that the Tasmanian tiger—a beloved symbol of the island state that appears on its license plate—has been extinct for nearly seven decades. But researchers behind that door are working to bring the animal back to life by cloning it, using DNA extracted from specimens preserved decades ago. Among other things, the work raises questions about the nature of extinction itself.

The Tasmanian tiger's Latin designation, *Thylacinus cynocephalus*, or "dog-headed pouched-dog," makes it redundantly clear that the marsupial's feline nickname is a misnomer. It comes from the dark striping on its back that runs nearly shoulder to tail. The animal had large, powerful jaws, which secured the predator a place atop the local food chain. Females carried their young in backward-facing pouches.

Thylacines, once spread throughout mainland Australia and as far north as New Guinea, were probably outcompeted for food by the dingoes that humans introduced to the area some 4,000 years ago, says Australian Museum director Mike Archer, founder of the cloning project. Eventually, thylacines remained only on the dingo-free island of Tasmania, south of the mainland. But with the arrival of European settlers in the 1800s, the marsupial's days were numbered. Blamed (often wrongly) for killing livestock, the animals were hunted indiscriminately. The government made thylacines a protected species in 1936, but it was too late; the last specimen reportedly died in captivity the same year.

The Australian researchers set out to bring the animal back partly to atone for humanity's role in its extinction, Archer says. The idea took root 15 years ago when he saw a pickled thylacine pup in the museum's collection. "It jarred me and started me thinking," recalls the 58-year-old paleontologist and zoologist, who received his undergraduate degree from Princeton University and his doctorate from the University of Western Australia. "DNA is the recipe for making a creature. So if there is DNA preserved in the specimen, why shouldn't we begin to use technology to read that information, and then in some way use that information to reconstruct the animal? I raised the issue with a geneticist. The response was derisive laughter."

Then, in 1996, Dolly the sheep burst onto the scene and, suddenly, Archer says, "cloning wasn't just a madman's dream." Dolly proved that DNA from an ordinary animal cell—in her case, a ewe's udder—could generate a virtually identical copy, or clone, of the animal after the DNA was inserted into a treated egg, which was implanted in a womb and carried to term. Archer's goal is even more ambitious: cloning an animal with DNA from long-dead cells, reminiscent of the sci-fi novel and movie *Jurassic Park*. The challenge? The DNA that makes up the chromosomes in which genes are bundled falls apart after a cell dies.

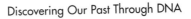

Researchers working with Don Colgan, head of the museum's evolutionary biology department, extracted DNA from a thylacine pup preserved in alcohol in 1866, and biologist Karen Firestone obtained additional thylacine DNA from a tooth and a bone. Then, using a technique called polymerase chain reaction, the researchers found that the thylacine DNA fragments could be copied. The scientists next have to collect millions of DNA bits and pieces and create a "library" of the possibly tens of thousands of thylacine genes—a gargantuan task, they concede. Still, an even greater obstacle looms, that of stitching all those DNA fragments together properly into functioning chromosomes; the scientists don't know how many chromosomes a thylacine had, but suspect that, like related marsupials, it had 14. But no scientist has ever synthesized a mammalian chromosome from scratch. If the Aussie scientists accomplish those feats, they may try to generate a thylacine by placing the synthetic chromosomes into a treated egg cell of a related species—say, a Tasmanian devil, another carnivorous marsupial—and implant the egg in a surrogate mother.

Such cross-species cloning, as the procedure is called, is no longer fantasy. In 2001, Advanced Cell Technology (ACT) of Worcester, Massachusetts, succeeded in cloning, for the first time, an endangered animal, a rare wild ox called a gaur. This past April, scientists from ACT, Trans Ova Genetics of Sioux Center, Iowa, and the Zoological Society of San Diego announced they had cloned a banteng, an endangered wild bovine species native to Southeast Asia, using a domesticated cow as a surrogate mother. Meanwhile, researchers in Spain are trying to clone an extinct mountain goat, called a bucardo, using cells collected and frozen before the species' last member died in 2000. Other scientists hope to clone a woolly mammoth from 20,000-year-old specimens found in Siberian permafrost.

Many scientists are skeptical of the thylacine project. Ian Lewis, technology development manager at Genetics Australia Cooperative Ltd., in Bacchus Marsh, Victoria, Australia, says the chances of cloning an animal from "snippets" of DNA are "fanciful." Robert Lanza, ACT's medical director and vice president, says cloning a thylacine is beyond existing science. But it may be within reach in several years, he adds: "This area of genetics is moving forward at an exponential rate."

In Australia, critics say the millions of dollars that the thylacine project will cost would be better spent trying to save endangered species and disappearing habitats. One opponent, Tasmanian senator and former Australia Wilderness Society Director Bob Brown, says people might become blasé about conservation if they're lulled into thinking a lost species can always be resurrected. The research "feeds the mind-set that science will fix everything," he says.

Another concern touches on the great nature-nurture quandary: Would a cloned thylacine truly represent the species, given that it would not have had the chance to learn key behaviors from other thylacines? For some carnivores, says University of Louisville behavioral ecologist

Lee Dugatkin, "it's clear that young individuals learn various hunting strategies from parents." And a foster parent might not fill the gap. Dugatkin asks whether a cloned Tasmanian tiger raised by a surrogate Tasmanian devil would just be a devil in tiger's clothing.

But Archer says, in effect, a thylacine is a thylacine, however its DNA blueprint is obtained, because much animal behavior, including that of marsupials, is genetically hardwired or instinctual. "We take kittens and raise them with humans, but they still behave like cats," he points out. And Archer, who envisions nature preserves populated by cloned thylacines and their offspring, says the project is actually a boon to conservation: it shows what it takes just to contemplate resurrecting a vanished species.

For now, Archer and coworkers are trying to piece together the thylacine's exact genetic makeup. That won't, of itself, bring the animal back, but it may provide new insights into the workings of the lamented creature. In that sense, the real danger would be not trying.

Originally published in *Smithsonian* (June 1, 2003). Reprinted with permission from Luba Vangelova.

2 Mutation, Adaptation, and Natural Selection

A mutation is any change to the sequence of nucleotides in a DNA molecule. Some genetic mutations are harmful, leading to disease. Others can actually prove beneficial, contributing to the long-term survival of an organism or species. British naturalist Charles Darwin offered the example of the giraffe's long neck, evolved to reach leaves on high tree branches, to illustrate the concept of natural selection. Natural selection is the process by which organisms with more desirable traits, that is, giraffes with longer necks in Darwin's example, were more likely to survive and pass those traits to their descendants than organisms that did not possess those traits.

Natural selection was always believed to follow random mutations, but molecular biologist and independent investigator Lynn Helena Caporale presents a novel theory: that some mutations actually occur strategically and for a purpose, in response to the pressures of natural selection. For example, exposure to bacteria *our ancestors never encountered can lead to changes in pieces of our DNA that help us produce special antibodies to fight against those bacteria. The organisms that evolve mutations that can respond to challenges in the environment will ultimately face the greatest odds of survival, she contends. —SW*

"Foresight in Genome Evolution"
by Lynn Helena Caporale
American Scientist, May–June 2003

When Charles Darwin and Alfred Russel Wallace remarked on the great variation among the individual members of so many species around the world, from pigeons to beetles, they could only imagine what the source of such variation might be. They certainly never heard of the double-helical structure of DNA or the sequence of a genome. Clearly, a great deal has come to light about the basis of heredity since their lifetimes. When evolutionary theory incorporated the notions of genes and mutation, biologists assumed that mutations are completely random because, as University of Utah biologists W. Joe Dickinson and Jon Seger recently wrote, natural selection "lacks foresight, and no one has described a plausible way to provide it." The process of evolution began to be described in terms of "random mutation" followed by natural selection. In this case, *random* can mean randomly distributed across a DNA sequence or random with respect to whether the change might be constructive or destructive, or both.

If the challenges that confronted genomes always were unprecedented and erratic, it would be hard to disagree with the statement that selection must lack foresight and mutations must be random with respect to their potential effect on survival. But certain types of challenges confront organisms over and over again. For example, our immune system is engaged in an arms race where it has to identify and dispose of pathogens while, in parallel, successful pathogens evolve to hide from our immune system. For challenges that recur, selection can favor mutation strategies that are better than random. This is not the same as knowing the precise genetic change that will overcome the challenge at hand, but mutation strategies that are better than random can provide a survival advantage compared to completely random mutation.

The probability of any given change in genome sequence, that is, of each mutation, reflects myriad biochemical properties encoded in that genome, from the accuracy of the proteins that copy and repair DNA to the availability of each of the DNA bases: adenine, thymine, guanine and cytosine (known as A, T, G and C). At a more local level, variations in the physical and chemical properties of a particular stretch of DNA sequence can have profound effects on the accuracy of the enzymes that rush past to copy it, at a rate of 80 to 500 bases each second, and on the systems that repair mismatched helices and DNA damage. Hence, the probability of distinct types of mutation varies intrinsically along a DNA sequence.

One striking example where the sequence context affects what mutations are likely involves the virus T4, which infects bacteria. A DNA letter insertion, deletion and two substitutions in a specific strip of the viral genome may appear to be random, but these mutations occur much more frequently than other changes. Close inspection reveals that the strands in that strip have a sequence that is almost a palindrome—a symmetrical sequence that reads the same from left to right on one DNA strand as from right to left on the complementary strand—and so each strand of the helix can loop out to pair with itself. The frequent mutations apparently result when the sequence forms a loop that is "corrected" to a more exact palindrome.

As our databases fill with the sequences of more and more genomes, the new "molecular" naturalists increasingly will discover variations among biochemical mechanisms that affect mutation, much as Darwin and Wallace found diversity among beaks and wings. Much like intrinsic variations in anatomical structures, intrinsic variations in the probability, type and location of genetic changes are subject to the pressure of natural selection, through the ways they affect the survival of their descendants. Darwin wrote, "[W]hy should we doubt that variations in any way useful to beings . . . would be preserved, accumulated, and inherited?" And so we can ask, why should we doubt that variations in the probability of particular types of mutations that may be useful to beings would thus be preserved, accumulated, and inherited?

A Genome's Implicit Range

Some mutations occur with a probability that is orders of magnitude higher than other mutations and in fact can fairly be called predictable; given a routine combination

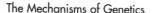

of time and population size, such mutations almost certainly will turn up. It is common to refer to one particular sequence of DNA as an organism's genome, and we expect that progeny of this organism normally inherit the same sequence, except when mutation intervenes. Yet within populations of only thousands of bacteria, certain mutations are predictable. For example, repeats such as CCCCC . . . or AGTCAGTCAGTCATGC . . . increase and decrease in length with notable frequency as the two strands of the double helix slip and misalign when the DNA is being copied or repaired.

In other words, among a population of bacteria that can trace their inheritance back to a single individual, a range of lengths of each mutable repeat in the genome will inevitably arise. Such mutations not only are predictable but are also reversible—reversible because, as these repeats continue to slide back and forth, the parental length will reappear regularly among the population of descendants. Therefore, the genome encodes more than a specific repeat length that can mutate. It actually encodes a specific repeat length explicitly and a range of repeat lengths implicitly. To say it another way, a *range* of lengths is an *inherited* property of the genome.

Changes in the lengths of repeats are more than a biochemical curiosity; they have biological consequences. They can affect how often a gene is transcribed or even shift the reading frame within a gene, which is translated three letters at a time. Frequent slips disrupt a gene's reading frame, damaging and occasionally resurrecting the function of the gene; a population of descendants will include both individuals with and individuals without active forms of the slippery gene. In *Neisseria meningitidis*, a species of bacteria that we carry in our throats and that can cause meningitis, the length of a string of Gs in a region promoting expression of the outer membrane protein porA affects the amount of the protein produced. Spacers of 11, 10 or 9 Gs lead, respectively, to high, medium or no detectable levels of expression.

The length of a repeat can also affect how sensitive a gene is to being turned on and off by specific molecules in its environment. In the case of one gene in the bacterium *Escherichia coli*, as a nearby string of Ts shortens in length from seven to three, the gene becomes less and less sensitive to one of the molecules that usually regulates its activity. Because their frequent changes in length tend to adjust gene activity, such repeats have been described as genomic "tuning knobs."

Natural selection has acted both on the location of slippery repeats in genomes and on their propensity for slipping. In the bacteria *Haemophilus influenzae* and *N. meningitidis*, genes associated with slippery repeats such as CAATCAATCAATCAAT . . . or CTCTTCTCTTCTCTT . . . include those that are involved in evading hosts' immune systems and in sticking to our various tissues; bacteria that can vary these properties quickly are likely to have a survival advantage and so be more "fit." The amount of diversity some species can generate through different combinations of repeat lengths is impressive; one genome survey of *Neisseria* suggests that there may be nearly 100 genes that have the potential to vary this way.

Natural selection can affect not only how frequently the repeats of a given gene change in length; it also can have genome-wide effects. The overall probability of slips can change when the proteins involved in copying DNA mutate, affecting the future probability of specific types of mutations at myriad places throughout the genome for generations. Another more complex reversible mutation is the graphically named "flip-flop" system in which a segment of DNA is cut out, inverted and pasted back into the helix. The orientation of this invertible piece controls whether the adjacent gene will be on or off.

The range of genomes encoded implicitly through the many possible combinations of repeat lengths and flip-flops extends the range of conditions in which a population can live; because of this flexibility, descendants are not committed to evolve along a path that only the circumstances of the moment may favor. Thus, although a genome encodes a single sequence, it can encode the ability to generate a predictable diversity of genomes among its descendants, extending their potential range. Its progeny inherit multiple sequences, one explicitly and others implicitly.

Ramping Up Evolution

When we think about natural selection, we think about, for example, selecting for a change in the genome that makes a bird's beak a little better at cracking seeds or enables a starving bacterium to digest an available sugar or to destroy a new antibiotic. But the potential reach of natural selection includes individual mutations that have genome-wide effects on the likelihood and type of subsequent genetic changes; for example, mutations in polymerase, an enzyme that copies DNA, can affect the tendency of repeats to shrink and grow.

Some genetic changes can be selected because they make it easier to add new information to a genome, over and over, whatever that information may encode. For example, bacteria have a selective advantage when they are able to share information with one another on mobile blocks of DNA, which may encode antibiotic resistance or the ability to take up and use new food sources. This ability is like building a bacterial Internet, in which genomes gain access to information that has evolved in other genomes. The enzymes and DNA recognition sites necessary to transfer genetic information between bacteria emerge under what has been termed "second order" selection, for they provide a selective advantage to generations of descendants that have access to myriad other traits on which selection can act more directly.

This movement of large blocks of DNA plays a role in bacterial evolution that dramatically rivals what we usually think of as mutations—changes in a single A, T, G or C along a strand of DNA. When a pathogenic strain of *E. coli* isolated from hamburger that sickened people in Michigan was compared with a harmless laboratory strain, there were 75,168 individual differences among their As, Ts, Gs and Cs, but the DNA that had come into the genome "sideways" through transfer of large blocks of DNA added up to 1.34 million base pairs that were unique to the pathogenic strain and that included information responsible for making people sick. Compared with bacteria that can survive starvation or new antibiotics only if they've hit a lucky change in their individual As, Ts, Gs and Cs, bacteria that have access to information that has evolved in other genomes have a clear selective advantage under stressful circumstances.

Pathogens and Hosts

Pathogens that are spread by mosquitoes and ticks have to float around in our blood so that they can be accessible to sipping insects that carry them to new "hosts." But blood can be a dangerous place for a pathogen, the equivalent of standing in the full glare of the immune system's searchlight. Because it takes the immune system a little time to get organized to recognize and attack a new pathogen, the microbe can hide by changing its coat regularly. Just when the immune system begins to attack invaders with, say, "blue" coats, some in the group have switched their coats to "yellow" and so survive. One pathogen that can exchange patches on the surface of its coat in this way is the spirochete (screw-shaped bacterium) that causes Lyme disease, *Borrelia burgdorferi*. The change in the surface protein does not rely on purely random mutation. Most changes distributed randomly in the genome would damage perfectly useful genes, whereas it is specifically changes in the coat protein that protect the spirochetes from the immune system. Natural selection has favored the evolution of biochemical machinery that recognizes portions of the genome coding for exposed regions in the surface protein and alters them. This changeable area is bracketed by conserved sequences—an exact repeat of 17 bases, TGAGGGGGCTATTAAGG—that apparently mark the zone subject to change.

The evolution of specialized machinery to abet adaptation is not confined to microorganisms. Animals such as cone snails, scorpions and snakes evidently also use focused variation to generate new components of their venom.

People, too, can change blocks of DNA around in a strategic way, for example when we generate a diverse collection of antibodies to fight the unknowable range of pathogens that may intrude on our bodies. In the genomes we inherit from our parents, our antibody genes are encoded in unassembled pieces, as if our parents went to sleep before putting together a holiday gift. The antibody-making kit we inherit includes a selection of pieces of DNA, called variable regions, each of which encodes the ability to bind to something different, such as a portion of a particular pathogen. We also inherit specific tags that mark these *variable regions* in our genome as well as enzymes that recognize the tags. In cells that later give rise to antibody-producing cells, these enzymes cut the variable regions out of storage, one at a time, and paste them into another location in the DNA where they can be actively expressed, as part of our antibody molecules, when our bodies encounter a pathogen that the particular variable region recognizes.

When the pathogen-binding variable regions are relocated, they are inserted into a location in the genome that has an interesting feature: DNA placed here experiences a higher mutation rate than DNA at other spots in our genome. Even within the relocated DNA, mutations are not distributed randomly. The higher chance of mutation is focused on the very parts of the pathogen-binding region that code for the cavity involved in holding onto a pathogen. In other words, a mechanism has evolved that focuses mutations at hotspots where such variation can generate diverse antibodies.

It is possible to change the location of the mutation hotspots experimentally by altering the DNA sequence of the variable regions. Such experiments show that the tendency to have high mutation rates in a particular region is embedded in the genome in two ways: Some contexts have a high mutation rate, and specific hotspot sequences tend to be mutated when placed in that context.

The infrastructure that creates the great variation in our immune system emerged through *second-order* selection—that is, not just by selecting for each antibody one by one, but rather by selecting for the ability to generate a whole repertoire of antibodies, with variable regions that have the potential to bind to and protect us against new pathogens that our ancestors never encountered. Our immune systems must have such an ability, because the pathogens are evolving too.

Not all the antibodies that the immune system generates will protect us, so in that sense our antibodies contain a great deal of random variation. Yet their diversity relies on mutations that are not randomly distributed throughout the genes encoding the antibodies. In evolution only some variations may be favored by natural selection, but that does not mean that we can assume that variations are all generated by completely random processes.

Biologists are only beginning to understand the biochemistry of how our immune system focuses mutations in useful places. An enzyme that scans variable regions in their relocated homes may recognize and damage specific hotspot sequences in the DNA. The damaged sequences may then be "repaired" in a sloppy way, resulting in targeted mutations. This sloppy repair process draws on mechanisms that the genome uses regularly to repair other DNA sequences that are somehow damaged, for example because of chemical effects or exposure to radiation.

In fact, the rate of mutation in a genome is affected by the interaction of many biochemical activities. As Evelyn Witkin, formerly of Rutgers University, put it, "[T]he prevailing notion [used to be] . . . that mutations were instantaneous events . . . [T]he mutagen went 'zap!' and that was that." However, the location and probability of distinct mutations depend on both the genome's sequence and on the cell's specific biochemical environment—including the full complement of genes expressed—at the time genetic changes take place.

Genomes vary a great deal in their sensitivity to specific types of damage. Some genomes survive in conditions that seem to be inescapably damaging. For example, the bacterium *Deinococcus radiodurans* was first discovered living in an irradiated can of meat. The stability of the DNA of organisms living in hot springs also depends on mechanisms that repair and protect their DNA; otherwise, they would risk multiple mutations per gene every generation. But even outside what seem to be challenging environments, the mutation rate of any genome would be high without mechanisms that repair spontaneous damage, such as when bases fall off or lose pieces at body temperature.

If the ability to promote variation can evolve at sites ranging from those that encode bacterial coats to those encoding portions of our immune system, such facilitated adaptation is likely to be important in other locations that still await discovery.

Theme and Variations

Sometimes the best way for an organism to evolve a new ability is to make a copy of a gene that already is in the genome and to tinker with the duplicate. Starting with a gene that already does something useful is like starting close to the finish line. Families of genes that are related to one another have evolved this way, by copying and tinkering, thereby directing the capabilities already evolved in one gene toward a new target. For example, if a gene encodes the ability to detect one color of light, a gene that encodes the ability to detect a different color of light could evolve through small variations in a copy of the original light-detector gene. Some gene families have as many as 1,000 members; the process of duplication and alteration is an efficient route to useful new genes.

Does the "tinkering" that generates new members of gene families involve altogether random changes, or is it possible that, much like the mutation hotspots in antibodies' pathogen-binding regions, selection favors hotspots for change within particular portions of the duplicated genes? Perhaps parts of a duplicated gene that direct it against a specific function are more likely to change, whereas the shared function of the gene family members may be shielded from mutation. Consistent with this idea, the rates of distinct types of genetic changes are in fact unevenly distributed across the mammalian genome, but the link between the uneven distribution of mutations and its biological sources and effects remains to be investigated.

Another interesting facet of genomes is the fact that there is more than one way to encode almost every amino acid. The genetic code is called *degenerate* because there are 64 possible three-letter units of DNA available to code for only 20 amino acids. This fact allows additional information to evolve in a DNA sequence along with the information specifying an amino acid sequence. For example in the spirochete that causes Lyme disease, a unit of five amino acids (glutamate-glycinealanine-isoleucine-lysine) is repeated in coat proteins; an enzyme recognizes the DNA that encodes this repeated unit in order to vary patches that allow the Lyme bacterium to change its coat. Because of the degeneracy of the genetic code, the five amino acids can be encoded, theoretically, in nearly 200 different ways, yet only one of these 200 choices is used. If the DNA sequence changes to one of the nearly 200 others, the amino acids may not change, but the DNA patch-varying machinery will no longer be able to be directed to the right spot in the genome where it can act to change the spirochete's coat.

Foresight Emerges via Experience

The number of distinct ways any genome might mutate randomly is vast. But the pressures of natural selection, generation after generation, can increase the chance that individuals with a fortuitous tendency to make certain biologically useful mutations survive. In other words, natural selection can act on variations in the probability of different types of mutations in different places in the genome much as it can act on variation in beaks and wings. For example, biochemical systems that enable the movement of intact pieces of DNA between bacteria have been selected as more useful than random changes in DNA sequence. Genomes that intrinsically tend to make changes that turn out to be more adaptive tend to have more surviving progeny, generation after generation, than randomly mutating genomes.

I want to emphasize that saying that, through natural selection, mutation can become no longer random is not the same as claiming that a genome will *know* that if it replaces a particular A with a G, it will be able to digest a specific sugar. Certainly, what I have said does not imply that all mutations are not random with respect to function, or that all mutations are helpful.

Still, some genomes have evolved that encode not just one "explicit" sequence, but rather a cloud of what

I have called implicit genomes, which gives their progeny access to a combinatorial assortment of properties in a way that is reversible across generations. This endows descendants with the ability to tolerate a range of environmental conditions that is wider than the range of the explicit genome. Further, genomes can gain access to additional, intact information through mechanisms that move DNA within and between genomes.

Genomes actively generate diversity, for example through the cutting and pasting of chromosomes during the formation of mature sperm and eggs, for there is an advantage to diversity in itself. The community will be more likely to survive the sweep of a new pathogen if individuals are different from one another. Similarly, if the food supply or the environment changes, diversity can protect the population against the new pressures.

Genomes cannot predict the future any more than we can, but based on what has happened to us in the past, genomes, like us, learn about what is likely to happen in the future. Mechanisms that diversify and stabilize the genome themselves feel the pressure of natural selection. The ability to anticipate recurring challenges is in fact a major challenge of evolution.

From the variation in bacterial surface proteins to the vertebrate immune response, it is clear that a great deal of genetic change is generated in a way that is better than random in its potential effect on survival. Indeed, as I have argued, some potentially useful mutations are so probable that they can be viewed as being encoded implicitly in the genome. As we examine our genomes and those of our fellow creatures, I anticipate evolutionary theory will evolve to include the under-standing that under selective pressure, the probability of different classes of mutation can change, with conse-quences for survival.

Reprinted with permission from *American Scientist*.

In the 1850s, an Austrian monk named Gregor Mendel began conducting his now-famous cross-breeding experiments with pea plants. He described the process by which certain traits (which we now call genes) are inherited from generation to generation. Mendel's studies laid the groundwork for the principles of inheritance underlying all future genetic research.

According to Mendel's idea, a single varia-tion in a single gene leads to a particular trait or disease. But scientists now know that traits occur as the result of interactions between many differ-ent genes. Both biological and environmental conditions can influence the effects of certain genes. In this article, Duke University biologist Frederik H. Nijhout focuses on these so-called complex traits. He shows why two people with the same disease gene may not both get the disease. Whether a person who carries a disease gene actually develops the disease may also depend upon the influences of his or her genetic background and environment.

Nijhout and his colleagues are working to develop a mathematical modeling method to help them analyze the association between genetic and environmental variables and to better understand how genes interact in a complex system. —SW

"The Importance of Context in Genetics"
by Frederik H. Nijhout
American Scientist, **September 1, 2003**

In the early days of genetics, scientists thought that each gene coded for a single trait, such as color, shape or size. This belief arose from the 19th-century work of Gregor Mendel, the father of genetics, who by design or serendipity studied traits whose variation was due almost entirely to variation of a single gene. Consequently, Mendel was able to perceive basic patterns that illustrate the fundamental laws of heredity.

As our experience with genetics grew, it became clear that most traits, or *phenotypes*, are inherited in more complicated ways than Mendel had described. This is because differences between the traits of any two individuals are almost always due to differences in many genes. The isolated effect of a single gene is typically observed only with carefully controlled breeding experiments, or in those rare cases where one gene is so badly damaged that its absence overwhelms the variation in other genes that affect the phenotype.

When many genes contribute to a trait, it can be difficult to discern each gene's contribution to the final result. Moreover, when many of the genes vary from individual to individual, the inheritance pattern of the trait can become exceedingly complex. Indeed, the term *complex trait* is used to describe a trait whose inheritance from generation to generation does not obey Mendel's rules.

One way to understand the inheritance of complex traits is by analyzing the biochemical mechanisms by which genes effect a phenotype. Below, I discuss the general nature of complex genetic traits and illustrate how their inheritance can be visualized with simple graphs that show how interactions among many genes can control one trait. This visualization provides a key to an intuitive understanding of complex inheritance and helps explain why having a disease gene cannot always predict disease risk.

Flowers and Phenotypes

Mendel showed that crossing a pure-breeding white-flowered pea with a pure-breeding violet-flowered pea always yielded progeny with violet flowers. Interestingly, when these violet-flowered offspring were crossed with each other, one-quarter of the progeny were white flowered, and the rest were violet. This observation is explained by the fact that each individual inherits one version of a gene, called an allele, from each of its parents and passes one of these along to each of its offspring. This genetic composition is referred to as an individual's *genotype*. In this case, the allele for violet color is dominant over that for white color, so when the two alleles occur together the flower is always violet. There is an equal probability that an offspring will receive one or the other allele from each parent, and this accounts for the fact that two violet-flowered parents can have white-flowered offspring.

All of the traits Mendel studied are examples of *discontinuous phenotypes*—white or violet flowers, round or wrinkled peas, tall or short stems. In each case there were two alleles per gene, and one of them was completely dominant over the other. However, it doesn't always work this way, even for traits that appear to be governed by a single gene.

Consider the inheritance of color in snapdragon blossoms, first described by Erwin Baur near the beginning of the 20th century at what is now the Max-Planck-Institut für Züchtungsforschung. As in pea flowers, the color of snapdragon flowers depends on a single gene with two common alleles—red and white. But in this case neither is dominant: Crossing a pure red- with a pure white-flowered plant gives progeny with pink flowers. That is, the combination of red and white alleles gives an intermediate result, a phenomenon also known as incomplete dominance, which can be readily seen because snapdragon flower color is a *continuous phenotype* with (potentially) a continuous range of pinks between white and red.

Simple Traits and Rate-Limiting Steps

Snapdragons provide an example of a common finding, that many traits are continuously variable within a population. In a few cases this is because of variation in a single gene, but the vast majority of traits are affected by many genes. In fact, even flower color is a product of several underlying genetic causes.

Many genes control pigment biosynthesis in flowers. Some of these genes code for enzymes that transform colorless precursors, such as amino acids and sugars, into variously colored pigments. These biosynthetic pathways can include more than a dozen steps, each regulated by a different enzyme. Other genes code for proteins that regulate enzyme synthesis and activity; these regulators affect the time and place where pigments are produced. Yet other proteins control the stability and subcellular localization of the pigments. The genes that code for these regulatory proteins are, in turn, regulated by another set of proteins, called transcription factors, which are each encoded by a different gene. Still other genes control the production of transcription factors. This kind of interminable regression of regulation and interaction among genes may seem odd at first sight, but appears to be the rule, even for the simplest of traits.

How then is it possible for a single gene to appear to control the properties of a trait? One relatively straightforward way this can happen is if the enzyme encoded by that gene acts as the rate-limiting step: the point in any system that most impedes the flow through the system. Imagine water flowing sequentially through three different sized funnels. What determines the rate of flow through this series? Obviously, the narrowest funnel.

To apply this . . . to an understanding of genotypes and phenotypes, imagine that each of the funnels represents the action of a single enzyme in a metabolic pathway. High activity levels—which could reflect abundant protein, or high efficiency, or precise targeting within the cell—correspond to wide openings, whereas low activity levels are represented by narrow passages.

We can expand this illustration to explain why the inheritance of flower color appears to be controlled by a single gene, even though a great many genes are required for the correct synthesis of the pigment. [Imagine that] water represents precursor molecules that pass through sequential steps in a process that leads to pigment formation. Each funnel represents one gene product—the narrower the funnel opening, the lower the activity of that enzyme. If the product of Baur's red/white gene is the narrowest funnel in the series, the overall rate of pigment formation will be a function of its activity. As long as no other gene product has a lower activity, variation in this one gene will appear to control variation in flower color.

What happens when the activity levels of the other genes in the pathway fluctuate? In this simple model, nothing—as long as they don't approach the rate-limiting step. If one of the other steps in the pathway becomes rate limiting, then the red/white step will no longer solely determine the flower color. If another gene codes for a defective enzyme that effectively blocks the pathway (a so-called null mutation), the red/white allelic composition becomes irrelevant in the determination of flower color. The term for this effect, in which one gene alters the apparent effect of another gene, is *epistasis*.

Thus even in this simple example, the effect of a given gene on a trait can be sensitive to other genes in the pathway.

Our [mental picture] can also explain the dichotomous traits in Mendel's pea flowers. A binary phenotype only requires the addition of a discriminator to sense a threshold. [Imagine that] the discriminator is shown as a balance. If flow through the system is under the threshold, one phenotype manifests itself; exceeding the threshold by any margin yields another phenotype.

Mutations and Modifiers

A common way to study the relationship between a gene and a trait is to examine the effects of naturally occurring or artificially induced mutations of that gene. Most mutations diminish the activity of a gene product, and the effects of such a mutation can give clues about the normal role the gene plays in giving rise to the trait.

Over the years biologists have learned that the effect of a given genetic mutation on a trait is not an intrinsic property of the gene. The nature of the effect depends strongly on the cellular context in which the gene is expressed. For instance, Sean Carroll and his associates at the University of Wisconsin showed that in caterpillar embryos, the localized expression of the gene *distalless* induces the formation of legs. Expression of the same gene later in development, in the developing wing, induces the formation of a colored eyespot pattern.

The importance of context is also illustrated by studies on the effects of "knockouts" of specific genes in mice, a method that completely eliminates the function of a gene's product. For example, knockout of a retinoblastoma-related gene causes severe abnormalities and embryonic death in one strain of mice, but the same mutation in another strain has no effect: The mutant mice are viable and become fertile adults, as shown by Michael Rudnicki and his colleagues at McMaster University.

Other examples of the importance of context come from the study of cancer genetics. Mutations in genes that regulate normal cell growth and cell division can cause this regulation to go awry, resulting in the uncontrolled growth we recognize as cancer. Such mutated alleles are called oncogenes. Whether or not a particular oncogene actually causes cancer often depends on the genetic background of the individual, as well as particular environmental variables such as vitamin deficiency or smoking habits. When an oncogene is introduced into a mouse by genetic engineering, it typically induces cancer in only a few tissues, even when the gene is expressed broadly. This suggests that only some tissues provide the conditions that are necessary for the defective gene to have its deleterious effect.

Additivity and Why It's Wrong

The variable effects of oncogenes are usually attributed to so-called "contributing factors" that vary by tissue and individual. The identities of these factors are usually unknown. The simplest hypothesis is that each factor that affects a trait has a minute effect by itself, and that the sum of these small effects produces a large, observable influence on the phenotype.

We can call this idea the *additivity hypothesis*. If it were correct, we could make a catalog of the independent effects of each allele of every gene and use the information to deduce the effect of various allelic combinations. To the genetic sum we could add the numerical consequences of environmental factors, yielding a precise phenotypic description. If the trait of interest were a disease like cancer, the additivity hypothesis would allow us to determine, for each individual, whether or not that disease will occur based on knowledge of all contributing factors.

In reality, we do not know all the contributing factors, so we can only calculate the probability of disease. These probabilities come from statistical analysis of a large group of people, some of whom have the disease. Correlating the incidence of disease with each suspected contributing factor predicts the risk associated with the presence of that factor. The probabilities are thus not really predictions; they are a statistical description of that specific study group. The only safe prediction that can be made is that in *identical* groups, the correlations and probabilities will be approximately the same.

But even if we were to measure all the contributing factors, everything we know about the mechanisms by which genes affect traits suggests that a simple additivity hypothesis must be wrong. For starters, genes exert their influence through complex and highly interconnected networks of protein interactions, so the effects of any one player on the outcome of the whole integrated system are very indirect. An example is the

gene-regulatory network in early fruit fly development
. . . Here the gene products themselves regulate gene expression, controlling the degree to which some other protein, often another regulator, will be produced. In such complex networks, with branching and converging pathways, positive and negative feedback regulation, the effects of variation in one component are unlikely to interact additively with variation in other components.

Perhaps the most important reason why genetic effects are not additive is that the relation between genetic variation and trait variation is nonlinear. Nonlinearity results because the effect of genetic variation is context dependent, and this makes the effect of simultaneous variation at several genes difficult to predict. To understand the properties of nonlinear genetic systems we can begin with a simple example, namely the origin of dominance among the alleles of a gene in a hybrid individual.

Nonlinearity and Dominance

Nonlinearity simply means that an output is not a straight-line function of an input. The existence of dominant and recessive alleles in Mendel's peas is an example. In the pea flower [example], the existence of a discriminator, the scales, prevents the output from varying continuously with input. Not surprisingly, dominance is usually a result of nonlinear processes (such as thresholds) in biochemistry and development. A well-known example of how nonlinearity produces dominance comes from biochemistry, pointed out in

1981 by Henrik Kacser and James Burns at the University of Edinburgh. Kacser and Burns described how the overall rate of a series of enzyme-catalyzed reactions depended on the activity of one of the enzymes in the chain. The overall rate depends on how many enzymes there are in the chain. For a single-enzyme system, the rate of the reaction is simply a linear function of enzyme activity. But if there is more than one enzyme in the chain, the rate of the reaction (or flux through the pathway, as it is usually referred to) becomes a nonlinear function of the activity of any one of the enzymes, and this nonlinearity becomes increasingly pronounced as the chain becomes longer . . .

Let's examine one of the enzymes in such a reaction chain. Assume that the gene that codes for this enzyme has two alleles, and that the enzymes encoded by these two alleles have different activities. *Homozygotes* are defined as having two identical copies of one or the other allele; in this case, they define the lower and upper limits for enzyme activity in an individual. *Heterozygotes* will have one copy of the low-activity allele and one copy of the high-activity version, meaning that the total activity of the enzyme in a heterozygote will be exactly halfway between the activities of the homozygotes. But because flux through the pathway is not a linear function of enzyme activity, the flux in the heterozygote will be more like that of one of the two homozygotes. One of the alleles will appear to be dominant with respect to the other.

The important thing to recognize here is that dominance is not a property of the allele itself, because at the single-enzyme level the alleles act in a simple additive manner. Dominance arises out of context—in this case, the chain of reactions in which the enzyme is embedded. Dominance is thus a property of the system as a whole.

Variability in Multiple Pathway Steps

In calculating how a single enzyme's activity relates to overall reaction rate, Kacser and Burns assumed that the activities of all other enzymes in the pathway were constant. In a real biological system this is highly unlikely. Over thousands of generations, most if not all enzymes in a reaction chain will have accumulated genetic variation. So let us imagine what would happen if there is genetic variation in two of the enzymes in a pathway. Because we now have two independent variables, we can no longer represent the relation with a line graph; instead, the relation becomes a three-dimensional surface. We'll call it the phenotypic surface because it describes how the phenotype is related to genetic variation.

Each point on the phenotypic surface represents the combined effect of two independent variables. The dependent variable—phenotype—is equivalent to the flow or flux through the pathway. It is possible for two points (or two individuals) to have the same phenotypic value but very different genotypes. Here the degree of dominance of one gene can be seen also to depend on the alleles present at the other variable gene. If the second gene codes for enzymes with high activity the nonlinear relationship between the first gene and flux is different from what it would be in the presence of low activity. Again, the dominance of an allele is not intrinsic; it is an emergent property of the system—in this case, a function of exactly where on the phenotypic surface the individual resides.

Suppose there is no genetic variation: Each gene has but a single allele, and all individuals in a population are homozygous for every gene. There exists only a single genetic value for each gene, and all individuals in the population occupy the same point on the phenotypic surface. Now we can ask, if a mutation occurs in one of the genes, what effect will that have on the phenotype? The answer is that this will depend both on how big an effect the mutation has and on exactly where on the phenotypic surface the population is clustered. Let us assume the mutation has a large effect on one of the genes, the deletion of an inhibitory region, which maximizes the activity of the encoded enzyme. This mutation moves the individual to another point on the surface along a line parallel to the axis representing the mutated gene. If the individual is in an area of the landscape with a steep slope, the mutation will result in a much bigger phenotypic change than if the landscape were gently sloped. So the effect of mutation on a trait, just like the trait's dominance, depends on exactly where it is on the phenotypic landscape. In other words, the effect is not a property of the mutation itself, but a function of the entire system.

The Phenotypic Landscape

Now we are in a position to understand why mutations can have such different effects in different genetic backgrounds. The genetic background defines where on a phenotypic landscape an individual or population is located. [Imagine a phenotypic surface that] shows this surface with two individuals, X and Y, who have the same phenotype (on the same contour of the map) despite having different alleles for genes A and B. Because of their relative positions on the surface, mutations in gene A will have different consequences for Y (big phenotypic effect) than for X (negligible effect). The opposite will be the case for a mutation in gene Y.

We can imagine, then, that a population of individuals with genotype X could accumulate many mutations in gene A that would have little or no effect on the trait and would therefore not be removed by selection. An evolutionary biologist would call those "neutral" mutations. But mutations in the B gene would have a big effect on the trait, and if this change reduced the fitness of its bearer, such mutations would be removed by natural selection. Thus we have a situation in which genetic variation in one gene can be allowed to accumulate, while genetic variation in the other gene is selected against, even though both genes code for enzymes in the same biochemical pathway and, if they were studied in isolation, would appear to have equivalent effects on the trait.

As before, the opposite would be true for a population of individuals with genotype Y. Here, mutations in gene A would have little effect and appear to be neutral, whereas mutations in gene Y would have a bigger effect and would thus likely to be selected against. The severity of a mutation, from neutral to profound, is not a property of the mutant allele itself; it is determined by the alleles of other genes that the individual (or population) possesses.

Real Landscapes Are Multidimensional

A phenotypic surface is just a visual depiction of the processes that give rise to a trait. We have seen how surfaces can be constructed for a simple biochemical pathway. In principle, it is possible to extend this to any of the variables that influence a trait. There are three prerequisites: knowing the processes underlying the trait, writing the equations that represent those processes and graphing the equations to form a phenotypic surface. In practice this is a formidable task, for the moment largely limited to biochemical systems owing to the need for accurate mathematical descriptions of reaction kinetics. However, the last decade has produced great advances in understanding the genetic mechanisms of development, and some traits, such as the early embryonic development of *Drosophila melanogaster*, are being described with accurate mathematical models.

Biology is advancing at an extraordinary pace, and we can expect that many other traits will become sufficiently well understood to enable mathematical encapsulation. Real traits are affected by independent variation in many genes, requiring a multidimensional phenotypic surface with as many orthogonal axes as there are independent variables. For a computer it is not particularly difficult to deal with n-dimensional surfaces and their slopes, but these shapes are impossible to depict on paper. For purposes of visualization we typically deal with only two independent variables at a time, recognizing all along that these are embedded within a larger multidimensional framework.

Individuals and Populations

If individuals can be represented as points on a phenotypic surface, then populations are represented as clouds of points. The dispersion of such a cloud in different directions is then a representation of the allelic variation present in a population for each of the genes defining the trait. Different populations would occur in different regions of the surface, and if we know the shape of the phenotypic surface we can understand intuitively how mutations will affect a trait across a given population—which portion of the group is more vulnerable to perturbation by a given variable and which is resistant to the same change. Moreover, we would be able to study how different populations are dispersed on the surface and how populations move across the surface over time because of new mutations and natural selection.

Populations that have different optimal phenotypes will settle on different contours of the landscape. Once on a contour of optimal phenotype, it is unlikely that a population will spread out along that contour, because interbreeding among individuals that are distant from each other along the contour will produce intermediate phenotypes, which because of the nonlinearity of the system, are no longer on that same contour. Those individuals would be selected against, constraining the spread of genotypes along a contour. We can thus predict that populations will form relatively compact clusters of points on a phenotypic surface—at least until other variables appear that change the landscape or create new evolutionary pressure.

The Effect of Environment

One of the advantages of developing a quantitative mathematical description of a phenotype is that it allows us to incorporate all factors that can affect the development and properties of that phenotype. We need not be restricted to the effects of genes or enzymes; we can also take into account the effects of nongenetic factors such a temperature, nutrient supply and hormones secreted in response to external stimuli. These environmental factors will affect the rates of certain reactions or will introduce new interactions not present before, and their effects can be described by mathematical equations as easily as we plot the influence of a gene.

For instance, a 10-degree increase in temperature can double the rate of some biochemical reactions while inhibiting others, and this can have non-intuitive consequences for the overall operation of a complex biochemical pathway. By mathematically modeling such processes, the effect of temperature on reaction rates can be explicitly calculated. In the graph of such a system, temperature variation would be represented by an independent axis, orthogonal to all the other axes. Now the shape of the phenotypic surface is determined by both genetic and environmental variables, and we can examine exactly how the environment affects the sensitivity of the system to mutations in various genes.

When a trait changes in response to an environmental variable, the trait is said to exhibit *phenotypic plasticity*, and the graph that describes exactly how the trait changes in response to that variable is called a *reaction norm*. Thus in a phenotypic landscape, a section parallel to an environmental axis of variation represents the reaction norm for a given genotype, whereas one parallel to a genetic axis of variation represents the effect of mutations on a trait in a given environment.

It should be clear from all the foregoing that if the landscape is not flat and linear (and it probably never is), the effects of environment would be just as context dependent as the effects of genes.

Coda

In this graphical visualization of the phenotypic landscape, I have shown how the effect of a given gene can vary depending on the other genes that also control the trait. This dependence on context arises from nonlinearities in the processes underlying phenotypic expression. Even limited by the number of dimensions we can show on paper, an intuitive understanding of how genes interact in complex systems is possible. Multidimensional systems can be represented mathematically, and in the

The Mechanisms of Genetics

future, the development of computer-aided visualization methods that allow the user to move easily within a multidimensional space may well enable us to obtain even greater insights into these complex phenomena.

Reprinted with permission from *American Scientist*.

The Human Chromosome

3

Every cell in the human body contains twenty-two autosomes and two sex chromosomes. The sex chromosomes determine whether a developing embryo will become a male or a female. A female is designated by the sex chromosomes XX, whereas a male is designated by XY. During embryonic development, a region on the Y chromosome called SRY (sex-determining region Y) initiates the biochemical processes that lead to the production of the testes, making the embryo male.

What authors Karin Jegalian and Bruce T. Lahn want to know is, why are all of our twenty-two pairs of chromosomes identical, yet the sex chromosomes (X and Y) so different? Jegalian (a science writer at the National Institutes of Health) and Lahn (a researcher of the Howard Hughes Medical Institute and a professor in the Department of Human Genetics at the University of Chicago) both finished their doctoral research in the laboratory of geneticist David C. Page at the Whitehead

Institute for Biomedical Research in Cambridge, Massachusetts, and the Massachusetts Institute of Technology. Jegalian and Lahn follow the evolution of the sex chromosomes to reveal the processes by which the Y has lost some of its material over time and the ways in which it has compensated for the loss to both ensure a man's survival and protect his fertility. —SW

"Why the Y Is So Weird"
by Karin Jegalian and Bruce T. Lahn
Scientific American, February 1, 2001

Our X and Y chromosomes make an odd couple. The X resembles any other chromosome, but the Y—the source of maleness—is downright strange. How did the two come to differ so much?

The human chromosomes that determine sex—the X and Y—are a bizarre pair. The other 22 sets of chromosomes in our cells consist of well-matched partners, as alike as twin candlesticks. One chromosome in each duo comes from the mother and one from the father, but both are normally the same size and carry the same genes. (Genes are the DNA blueprints for proteins, which do most of the work in the body.) In stark contrast, the Y chromosome is much smaller than the X; in fact, it is positively puny. It harbors no more than several dozen genes, far fewer than the 2,000 to 3,000 on the X. A number of the Y genes have no kin at all on the X. And the Y is riddled with unusually high amounts of "junk" DNA: sequences of code letters, or nucleotides, that contain no instructions for making useful molecules.

Until recently, biologists had difficulty explaining how the Y fell into such disrepair. They had various theories but few ways to test their ideas. That situation has now changed, thanks in large part to the Human Genome Project and related efforts aimed at deciphering the complete sequence of DNA nucleotides in all 24 distinct chromosomes in humans—the X, the Y and the 22 autosomes (the chromosomes not involved in sex determination). Just as paleontologists can trace the evolution of a species by examining skeletons of living animals and fossils, molecular biologists have learned to track the evolution of chromosomes and genes by examining DNA sequences.

The new findings demonstrate that the history of the sex chromosomes has been strikingly dynamic, marked by a series of dramatic disruptions of the Y and by compensatory changes in the X. That interplay undoubtedly continues today.

Further, the Y chromosome—long regarded as a shambles, able to accomplish little beyond triggering the maleness program—turns out to do more than most biologists suspected. Over some 300 million years it has managed to preserve a handful of genes important for survival in males and to acquire others needed for fertility. Instead of being the Rodney Dangerfield of chromosomes (as some have called the chronically disrespected Y), the male chromosome is actually more like Woody Allen: despite its unassuming veneer, it wields unexpected power.

Sheer curiosity has driven much of the research into the evolution of the human sex chromosomes. But a more practical pursuit has informed the work as well: a desire to explain and reverse male infertility. Discoveries of Y genes that influence reproductive capacity could lead to innovative treatments for men who lack those genes or have defective versions.

The recent advances have benefited from insights achieved beginning about 100 years ago. Before the 20th century, biologists thought that the environment determined sex in humans and other mammals, just as it does in modern reptiles. For reptiles, the temperature of an embryo at an early point in development tips some poorly understood system in favor of forming a male or female. In the early 1900s, though, investigators realized that chromosomes can arbitrate sex in certain species. About 20 years later mammals were shown to be among those using chromosomes—specifically the X and Y—to determine sex during embryonic development.

Clues Piled Up

In the ensuing decades, researchers identified the Y as the male maker and deduced that the X and Y evolved from matching autosomes in an ancient ancestor. By chance, sometime shortly before or after mammals arose, a mutation in one small part of the autosome copy that would become the Y caused embryos inheriting that changed chromosome (along with its mate, the future X) to become males. Embryos inheriting two Xs became females.

In 1990 geneticists pinpointed the part of the Y that confers maleness. It is a single gene, named *SRY*, for "sex-determining region Y." The protein encoded by *SRY* triggers the formation of the testes, apparently by activating genes on various chromosomes. Thereafter, testosterone and other substances made in the testes take over the molding of maleness.

Scientists concluded that the human sex chromosomes started life as a matched pair in part because the tips of the X and Y have remained twinlike and able to engage in a process called recombination. During meiosis (the cell division that yields sperm and eggs), matching chromosomes line up together and swap segments, after which one copy of every autosome plus a sex chromosome is distributed evenly to each reproductive cell. Even though most of the Y now bears little resemblance to the X, the tips of those chromosomes align during meiosis in males and exchange pieces as if the X and Y were still a matching set. (Such alignment is critical to the proper distribution of chromosomes to sperm.)

Other evidence that the X and Y were once alike came from the part of the Y that does not recombine with the X. Many of the genes scattered through this nonrecombining region still have counterparts on the X.

The existence of the nonrecombining region, which makes up 95 percent of the Y, offered a clue to how that chromosome became a shadow of its original self. In nature and in the laboratory, recombination helps to maintain the integrity of chromosomes. Conversely, a lack of it causes genes in nonrecombining regions to accumulate destructive mutations and to then decay or disappear. It seemed reasonable to think, therefore, that something caused DNA exchange between large parts of the X and Y to cease, after which genes in the non-recombining region of the Y collapsed. But when and how recombination stopped after the Y emerged remained uncertain for decades.

Shaped in Stages

Work completed in the past five years has filled in many of the gaps. For instance, in 1999 one of us (Lahn) and David C. Page of the Whitehead Institute for Biomedical Research in Cambridge, Mass., showed that the Y lost the ability to swap DNA with the X in an unexpected, stepwise fashion—first involving a swath of DNA surrounding the *SRY* gene and then spreading, in several discrete blocks, down almost the full length of the chromosome. Only the Y deteriorated in response to the loss of X-Y recombination, however; the X continued to undergo recombination when two copies met during meiosis in females.

What could account for the disruption of recombination between the X and the Y? As the early X and Y tried to trade segments during meiosis in some far-distant ancestor of modern mammals, a part of the DNA on the Y probably became inverted, or essentially flipped upside down, relative to the equivalent part on the X. Because recombination requires that two like sequences of DNA line up next to each other, an inversion would suppress future interaction between the formerly matching areas of the X and Y.

We discovered that recombination ceased in distinct episodes when we examined the nucleotide sequences of 19 genes that appear in the nonrecombining region of both the X and the Y. (Some of the Y copies no longer function.) In general, if paired copies of a gene have stopped recombining, their sequences will diverge increasingly as time goes by. A relatively small number of differences implies recombination stopped fairly recently; a large number means it halted long ago.

Most of the X-Y pairs fell into one of four groups. Within each group, the X and the Y copies differed by roughly the same amount, indicating that recombination stopped at about the same time. But the groups clearly varied from one another. The Y copies that began diverging from their counterparts on the X at about the time the *SRY* gene arose differed from their partners the most, and the other groups showed progressively less divergence between the X and Y copies.

By comparing DNA sequences across species, biologists can often calculate roughly when formerly matching genes (and hence the regions possessing those genes) began to go their separate ways. Such comparisons revealed that the autosomal precursors of the X and Y were still alike and intact in reptiles that existed before the mammalian lineage began branching extensively. But monotremes (such as the platypus and echidna), which were among the earliest to branch off from other mammals, possess both the *SRY* gene and an adjacent nonrecombining region. These differences implied that the *SRY* gene arose, and nearby recombination halted, close to when the mammalian lineage emerged, roughly 300 million years ago.

We gained more information about the timing by applying a "molecular clock" analysis. Biologists can estimate the background rate at which DNA sequences are likely to change if they are under no particular pressure to stay the same. By essentially multiplying the extent of sequence disparity in X-Y pairs by that estimated rate, we deduced that the first recombination-halting inversion took place between 240 million and 320 million years ago.

Similar analyses imply that the next inversion occurred 130 million to 170 million years ago, shortly before marsupials branched off from the lineage that gave rise to all placental mammals. The third struck 80 million to 130 million years ago, before placental mammals diversified. And the final inversion rocked the Y roughly 30 million to 50 million years ago, after monkeys set off on their own evolutionary path but before apes and hominids parted company.

Bucking the overall trend for X-Y pairs, some genes in the nonrecombining region of the Y code for proteins that differ remarkably little from the proteins encoded by their X counterparts, even in the regions that underwent inversion earliest. Their preservation is probably explained by a simple evolutionary law: if a gene is crucial to survival, it will tend to be conserved. Indeed, the Y genes that have changed the least are mainly "housekeeping" genes—ones critically required for the integrity of almost all cells in the body.

Making Up for Losses

Logic—and a large body of research—indicates that the failure of recombination between the X and the Y, and the subsequent deterioration of many Y genes, must have been followed by a third process that compensated for the degeneration. The reasoning goes like this: Not all genes are active in every cell. But when a cell needs particular proteins, it typically switches on both the maternal and paternal copies of the corresponding genes. The amount of protein generated from each copy is fine-tuned for the optimal development and day-to-day operation of an organism. Therefore, as genes on the Y began to disappear, the production of the associated proteins would have been halved disastrously in males unless the affected species evolved compensatory tricks.

Many animals, such as the fruit fly, handle this inequity by doubling the activity of the X versions of lost Y genes in males. Others employ a more complex strategy. First they increase the activity of X genes in both males and females, a maneuver that replenishes protein levels in males but creates an excess in females. Some animals, such as the nematode worm, then halve the activity of X genes in females. Others, including mammals, invoke a process called X inactivation, in which cells of early female embryos randomly shut off most of the genes in one of their two X chromosomes. Neighboring cells may silence different copies of the X, but all the descendants of a given cell will display its same X-inactivation pattern.

Although X inactivation has long been thought to be a response to the decay of Y genes, proof for that view was lacking. If degeneration of Y genes drove X inactivation, then X genes having functional counterparts in the non-recombining region of the Y would be expected to keep working in females (that is, to evade inactivation)—so as to keep protein levels in females equivalent to those in males. In analyzing the activity levels of surviving X-Y pairs from two dozen mammalian species, one of us (Jegalian) and Page found a few years ago that the X copies of working Y genes do escape inactivation. Those analyses also revealed that X inactivation, although it happens in an instant during an animal's development today, did not evolve all at once. Instead it arose rather diffidently—patch by patch or perhaps gene by gene within a patch, not all at once down the chromosome.

Emerging Themes

Curiously, the nonrecombining region of the Y possesses not only a handful of valuable genes mirrored on the X but also perhaps a dozen genes that promote male fertility. The latter code for proteins made solely in the testes, presumably to participate in sperm production. Some seem to have jumped onto the Y from other chromosomes. Others have apparently been on the Y from the start but initially had a different purpose; they acquired new functions over time. Degeneration, then, is but one theme prominent in the evolution of the Y chromosome. A second theme, poorly recognized until lately, is the acquisition of fertility genes.

Theorists disagree on the forces that turned the Y into a magnet for such genes. The species as a whole may benefit from sequestering in males genes that could harm females or do nothing useful for them. It is also possible that being on the Y protects male fertility genes by ensuring that they go from male to male without having to detour through females (who could discard them without suffering any direct consequences).

Another mystery is how fertility genes can thrive in the absence of recombination, under conditions that corrupted most of the Y's other genes. An answer may lie in the observation that nearly every male fertility gene on the Y exists in multiple copies. Such amplification can buffer the effects of destructive mutations, which usually afflict just one copy at a time. As some copies accumulate mutations and eventually fail, the remaining ones continue to preserve a man's reproductive ability and to serve as seeds for their own multiplication.

The evolution of the sex chromosomes has been studied most thoroughly in humans. But together with cross-species comparisons, that research has identified general principles operating even in creatures that evolved sex chromosomes independently from mammals. Some of those animals, such as birds and butterflies, use the W-Z system of sex determination. When inheritance of a single copy of a specific chromosome leads to the formation of a male, that chromosome is termed the Y, and its partner is termed the X. When inheritance of one copy of a chromosome leads to the formation of a female, that chromosome is called the W, and its mate is called the Z.

One notable principle is that sex chromosomes derive from autosomes. The affected autosomes can vary, however. W and Z chromosomes in birds evolved, for example, from different autosomes than those that gave rise to the mammalian X and Y. And the X and Y in fruit flies derived from different autosomes than those enlisted by mammals.

In most sexually reproducing species, once sex chromosomes arose, they became increasingly dissimilar as they underwent one or more cycles of three sequential steps: suppression of recombination, degeneration of the nonrecombining parts of the sex-specific chromosome (the Y or W) and, finally, compensation by the other chromosome. At the same time, the sex-specific chromosome in many instances became important for fertility, as happened to the Y in humans and insects.

It is reasonable to wonder what the future holds for our own species. Might the cycle continue until it wipes out all recombination between the X and the Y and ultimately destroys the Y, perhaps thousands or millions of years from now? The new discoveries suggest males are able to protect Y genes that are critical for male survival and fertility. Nevertheless, total decay of the Y remains a theoretical possibility.

Research into genes is often undertaken with an eye to understanding and correcting human disorders. Some investigations into the Y chromosome began with just such a goal in mind-understanding male development and correcting infertility. But many studies were less focused on therapy. As more and more genes on the X and Y were identified by medical research and systematic sequencing efforts, evolutionary-minded scientists could not resist asking, on a more basic level, whether those genes had anything new to say about the distant past of the strangely mismatched X and Y chromosome. As it turns out, the genes had a rich tale to tell.

During the processes of mitosis and meiosis, a single cell divides into two genetically identical cells. Each cell receives a complete set of genetic material via the chromosomes. The centromere — the repetitive stretch of DNA inside the chromosome — is a little understood but very important player in this process. Before the cell divides, the chromosomes duplicate, and the centromere holds the duplicated pairs together until threadlike structures called spindle fibers separate them and the cell divides. If the centromere doesn't function properly, chromosome duplication can go awry, sometimes resulting in structural malformation or disease.

Until recently, scientists have known little about the centromere. Its twisting, repetitive stretches of DNA have made it very difficult to sequence. For many years, researchers were

able to sequence the centromere in yeast only because it was made up of a relatively short sequence of 125 bases. Compare that to the approximately 3 million bases in a human centromere.

But in this article, investigator Daphne Preuss and her colleagues at the University of Chicago have been able to learn more about the inner workings of the centromere in a plant—the mustard plant Arabidopsis. *The way in which* Arabidopsis *cells duplicate has enabled Preuss and her team to define the centromere region in a way never before possible. Preuss's team and other scientists studying the centromere have since discovered that its long stretches of genetic material are not just "junk" DNA, as was once believed, but actually contain active genes. Preuss expects to soon have all five* Arabidopsis *centromeres sequenced and hopes to gain a better understanding of the functioning genes within them.* —SW

"Centromeres: A Journey to the Center of the Chromosome"
by Christine Mlot
Science, December 15, 2000

As a postdoc at Stanford University in 1994, Daphne Preuss was examining mutagenized pollen grains under a microscope when she saw it: Amid all the dots of lone pollen, four grains were stuck together, tracing the shape of a tetrahedron. Having written her Ph.D. thesis on yeast, where such tetrads are standard and have been the foundation for its genetic analysis, Preuss knew she was looking at something powerful. "I immediately knew this [mutant] was the key to doing all kinds of genetic analysis" in plants, she recalls. "Life would be different."

That chance finding launched her career as a plant biologist. Some 6 months after she found it, an electron micrograph of the mutant pollen was on the cover of *Science* (3 June 1994), and Preuss was soon on her way to the University of Chicago, where she directs a lab that runs in large part on the power of her mutant find, dubbed *quartet*.

The lemon-yellow pollen grains in which she spotted quartet were from the mustard plant *Arabidopsis thaliana*. What was unusual was that the four gametes were joined. Typically during meiosis in a plant or animal, the two chromosomes within a cell join; recombine, or exchange genetic material; then divide and separate twice into four haploid cells—the gametes. Each gamete, whether pollen or sperm, contains half the genetic complement. But in this newfound *Arabidopsis* mutant, the standard diploid cell produces four adjoined haploid cells—a tetrad, as in yeast. By analyzing these four cells instead of random gametes, geneticists can chart recombination events with unprecedented precision. Preuss realized that this four-in-one mutant could reveal what happens during meiosis in plants as it had in yeast. It would also enable her to define the centromeres, which have been defined in yeast but which remain a black box in plants and animals.

The centromere is a crucial stretch of DNA buried in the knotty terrain at the center of the chromosome. It plays a key role in meiosis, pairing up parental chromosomes and hitching them to protein motors that pull the chromosomes apart before cells divide. The dense, central region of the chromosome containing the centromere is readily visible under a microscope. Yet only in yeast have researchers been able to identify the exact DNA sequence of the centromere.

Using the *Arabidopsis* tetrad mutants, Preuss has established where the centromeric region starts and stops on each of the five chromosomes, a first for a complex eukaryote. Now, by building "minichromosomes," she and her colleagues are on their way to pinpointing where and how in that region the proteins attach in meiosis. The research is "blazing trails," says Kelly Dawe of the University of Georgia, Athens, who is developing such minichromosomes in maize.

Preuss's lab and *quartet* have also been indispensable to the *Arabidopsis* genome sequencing project, started in 1996 with the goal of deciphering the plant's 120-million-base-pair sequence. The fine-scale genetic map her group developed by using pollen tetrads boosted the unprecedented accuracy and completeness of the sequence of this model organism. Not only did the map enable Preuss to define the centromeric region, but it also enabled the six sequencing groups to assign unknown fragments of DNA, especially from the centromeric region, to their rightful places on the chromosomes. "We wouldn't have been able to have done it without her and [postdoc] Greg Copenhaver," says W. Richard McCombie of the sequencing group at Cold Spring Harbor Laboratory in New York.

Into the Chromosome Centers

Under a microscope, the cinched region of the centromere is easily one of the most distinguishing features of the threadlike chromosomes. Indeed, cytologists captured the first images of the centromere in the late 1800s. But for all their centrality—literally and figuratively—in dividing cells, centromeres have escaped much dissection. "The centromere has been remarkably elusive to pin down," says Brian Charlesworth, an evolutionary biologist at the University of Edinburgh in the United Kingdom.

For decades both cell biologists and geneticists have attacked the problem of how chromosomes segregate and the role the centromere plays in this process. By the 1940s geneticists were mapping the locations of the dense centromeric regions in yeast and other fungi. This was possible because these organisms packaged their gametes in tetrads, which enabled geneticists to track recombination among the four cells. The centromeres always stayed put on the chromosomes they started out with, in contrast to other recognizable markers. Thus, the centromeres became the baseline for measuring distance to markers on the chromosome arms. From that point on, tetrad analysis became a

stock in trade for geneticists, especially as yeast became the favored model system.

In 1980, using tetrad analysis, researchers narrowed the location of the centromere to about a 4000-base stretch of DNA in budding yeast, the first organism to achieve that landmark at that level of resolution. Eventually, as molecular technologies improved, yeast's functional centromere—the precise bases involved in hitching chromosomes to the proteins—was whittled down to a 125-base stretch.

Meanwhile, during the 1960s and '70s, cell biologists had developed staining and other techniques that visually highlighted the centromeric region on the larger chromosomes of plant and animal cells. These techniques also highlighted the corresponding protein structure the centromere meshes with. By that time, researchers were beginning to realize that eukaryotes had devised many ways to segregate their chromosomes—in other words, one centromere did not fit all. But except in yeast, the exact DNA sequence of the centromeres remained elusive, escaping detection even in the massive projects to sequence the genomes of fruit flies and humans.

The problem is that the chromosome centers are jungles of difficult loops and repetitions, or heterochromatin, in contrast to the smooth runs of readable DNA, or euchromatin, on the chromosome arms. As sequencers—who decipher the genetic code of short fragments and then reassemble them in correct order— approach the central regions of the chromosomes, they run into long stretches of nothing but repeated bases, such as ATAT . . . AT. These stretches of repetitive DNA are next to impossible to piece together, as they contain few landmarks to orient them. The centromeric region is "the part of the genome that's ignored when it comes to estimating time to 'complete' genome projects," says Gary Karpen, who studies the centromere in *Drosophila* at the Salk Institute for Biological Studies in La Jolla, California.

In *Arabidopsis*, Preuss and her co-workers were able to find the right place for these "orphaned" stretches by analyzing the results of 1000 crosses using the mutant pollen, each cross producing four plants, one from each cell of the tetrad. With tetrads, "we can literally redraw what happened in meiosis," she says. They were able to find recognizable markers linked to these orphan stretches and then examine how often the markers stayed put with the centromeres in the tetrads generated in meiosis. The more often a marker separated from its centromere, the farther down the chromosome arm it was. The more often it stayed with its centromere, the closer in it was. The frequency of these separations, or recombinations, within a foursome was used to calculate distance between markers and centromeres. In this fashion the researchers generated successively finer scale maps of the genome, starting out with roughly one marker for every three megabases and finishing in the region of the centromere with one marker for every 10 kilobases. The frequency of recombination between a marker and its centromere also enabled the Preuss group to delineate where on the map the centromeric region starts and stops on all five chromosomes (*Science*, 24 December 1999, p. 2468). When they found no pattern of crossing over in the tetrads, the researchers knew that they had found markers in the genomic terra incognita of the centromeric region itself.

Among the five chromosomes, these genetically defined centromeric regions vary in length from 1.4 megabases to 1.9 megabases, says Preuss. That's about 7% of the entire genome—a far more precise definition of the *Arabidopsis* centromeric regions than earlier estimates of more than 40% of the genome, says Preuss. Inside these regions as well as flanking them, Preuss and her team found more repetitive sequences, most notably, recognizable sequences of 180 base pairs repeated hundreds of times, on all five chromosomes.

Surprising nuggets also turned up inside the centromeric regions, most notably, a significant number of genes. "That was one of the big interesting things," says Preuss, because the centromere had long been considered relatively barren territory. The analysis has located some 200 genes in the *Arabidopsis* centromeric regions, at least 50 of which are expressed. About 40 of these genes appear only once in the genome sequence. "These are bona fide genes that would have been left out" without delving into the centromeric region, says Preuss.

Creating Chromosomes

Having defined the centromeric regions and sequenced most of them, the researchers still need to find the functional part and figure out how it works. Given the diversity of centromeres in different organisms, there isn't a universal code to look for.

To find the functional centromere, Preuss's lab is developing a new tool— experimental minichromosomes that are a stripped-down version of an *Arabidopsis* chromosome. They contain all the essential parts: the centromere; telomeric DNA from the chromosome ends; genes of interest or indicator genes, such as green fluorescent protein; and elements to ferry the package into cells. When assembled, these minichromosomes should function in plants alongside the other chromosomes.

Postdoc Kevin C. Keith in Preuss's lab is now testing pieces of DNA from the *Arabidopsis* centromeric regions to see which ones work in cell division—the hallmark of a functional centromere. Keith is combing through all the bases in the centromeric region, including the 180-base repeats. The process is akin to going through jars of bolts in a hardware store to find the right one, in this case, a stretch of DNA that holds the minichromosome to the cell's protein motors. To do so, Keith is methodically inserting sequences of fewer than 100 kilobases into the minichromosomes to test which ones work as the centromere.

Such minichromosomes are in the works for other organisms, including humans. Apart from their use as a tool to explore chromosomal functioning, they have an applied side in genetic engineering as well. Researchers believe they will provide a controlled means of "stacking" large numbers of genes—say, for pathogen resistance— into an organism that could also be engineered to be eliminated when necessary.

One of Preuss's next interests is to use the minichromosomes to study why chromosomes don't always segregate properly and end up with two or no chromatids in a gamete instead of just one. If the gamete is used in fertilization, the resulting offspring will have an abnormal number of chromosomes, a condition known as aneuploidy. It happens between 1% and 2% of the time in *Arabidopsis*—about the same frequency as in yeast—but far more often in human meioses. The development of minichromosomes over the next 5 years "will open up tremendous resources" for exploring such phenomena, she says.

Preuss isn't the only one who thinks so. This past summer she became a Howard Hughes Medical Institute investigator, only the third plant biologist to be so recognized. To commemorate the occasion, Preuss's lab presented her with a framed collage of the pollen tetrads and the data they've generated. At the center is a photo of Howard Hughes holding a fistful of *Arabidopsis*. It's in bloom.

What Can Our DNA (and Animal DNA) Tell Us About Ourselves?

4

On April 25, 1953, two young scientists, James Watson and Francis Crick, reported in the journal Nature that they had discovered the structure of DNA. Scientists at the time already had an inkling that DNA was the material that held an organism's genetic information. Now they knew what it looked like. DNA, said Watson and Crick, resembled a spiral staircase, its rungs composed of pairs of chemical bases. They showed how the "double helix" was able to split apart to make an exact copy of its genetic material. Their article, though brief, would have profound and worldwide implications. Their discovery enabled scientists to see how genes passed from generation to generation, and it laid the groundwork for the modern science of genetics.

This article, written by Time editor at large Nancy Gibbs, commemorates the fiftieth anniversary of Watson and Crick's achievement. Its title comes from the now-famous pronouncement made by the pair of scientists as *they celebrated their discovery in a Cambridge, England, pub—"We have found the secret of life." Their words were no overstatement. As Gibbs shows, the DNA model has since revolutionized the fields of science and health care.*

Sadly, Francis Crick passed away in 2004, before the implications of his research had been fully realized. But, as Gibbs shows, his work will live on, as scientists continue to unravel all of the secrets held in DNA and use that knowledge to shape modern medicine. —SW

"The Secret of Life: Cracking the DNA Code Has Changed How We Live, Heal, Eat and Imagine the Future"
by Nancy Gibbs
Time, February 17, 2003

Any 4-year-old who likes ladybugs and lightning bolts can tell you that life is wildly beautiful as far as the eye can see. But it took the geniuses of our time to reveal how beautifully ordered life is deep down where we can't see it at all—in the molecular workshop where we become who we are. James Watson and Francis Crick did not discover the existence of DNA; they discovered its structure, which means they unveiled its power as well as its beauty. If you could uncoil a strip of DNA, it would reach 6 ft. in length, a code book written in words of four chemical letters: A, T, G and C. Fold it back up, and it shrinks to trillionths of an inch, small enough to fit in any one of our 100 trillion cells, carrying the recipe for how to make a human being from scratch. The ingredients are the same for everything that lives; we are cousins to sequoias, and slugs—one life, one creation.

"The molecule is so beautiful," Watson once observed in a chat with TIME. "Its glory was reflected on Francis and me," and the two scientists have spent their lives since then trying to live up to its standards. They marveled that something so vital could be so simple and such a surprise. When they toasted their discovery in a pub one February night 50 years ago, Watson and Crick had no idea that not only biology but also the drugs we take and the machines we build, the food we eat and the choices we face when we decide to have a baby would be changed forever by what they had found.

Now, at the golden anniversary, we celebrate how much we have learned since then, including how little we know. For years scientists thought we human beings must have about 100,000 genes stitched onto our 23 pairs of chromosomes, only to discover that the number is less than a third of that. Like a vaccine against pride, the sublime achievement of the human intellect reveals that we have only twice as many genes as a roundworm, about three times as many as a fruit fly, only six times as many as bakers' yeast. Some of those genes trace back to a time when we were fish; more than 200 come directly from bacteria. Our DNA provides a history book of where we come from and how we evolved.

It is a family Bible that connects us all; every human being on the planet is 99.9% the same.

On the other hand, we are learning that each letter in that text can spell the difference between blond and brunet, tall and short, life and death. A woman who carries a mutation in the BRCA1 gene can have a seven times greater chance of developing breast cancer. Scientists in Utah last week announced the discovery of a gene that seems to predispose carriers to depression. We are learning these things in part because of Watson, who, having revealed the simplicity of DNA's structure, wanted to explore the complexity of its function. He helped persuade Congress to fund the Human Genome Project, an attempt to decode the more than 3 billion letters of the complete human genome. Under competitive pressure from nimble private scientists, the goal was achieved ahead of schedule and under budget. In June 2000, when Bill Clinton and Tony Blair announced that the first rough draft of the genome was complete, Clinton declared that "without a doubt, this is the most important, most wondrous map ever produced by humankind." It was enough to fill 200 phone books at 1,000 pages each, or 75,490 pages of the *New York Times*. And it marked the turning point in the transformation of medicine from treating disease to preventing it altogether.

Each day now, as we discover where we are vulnerable, we move closer to designing drugs to protect us. Gene therapy allows doctors to introduce some handy gene into the body like a little rescue squad, to help produce enzymes that because of some faulty gene, the body can't make on its own. When we finally find cures for cancers, they will reflect the secrets of how our genes fight some cancers and yield to others. Drugs like Herceptin for breast cancer and Gleevec for leukemia work by blocking the chemical signal that tells the cancer to grow. They herald the day when we can look back on the traditional slashing and burning of cancer patients as having been as primitive as bloodletting.

And these new treatments are only a beginning. Genomics is already considered hopelessly 20th century by the scientists who have moved on to proteomics, the study of the proteins for which the genes provide the instructions. Since a typical gene may yield as many as 20,500 different kinds of proteins, scientists are only now figuring out how to begin to figure them out. Researchers don't even know how many proteins there are or how they fold, which means among other things that a whole new kind of machine is needed to study them. The new computers are coming to life. IBM models its newest ones—computers that act like cells and fix themselves wherever they break—after DNA. The quantity of information is so vast, we have to invent new numbers to measure it: not just terabytes (a trillion bits of genetic data) but petabytes (equivalent to half the contents of all the academic libraries in America), exabytes, yottabytes and zettabytes. All the words ever uttered by everyone who ever lived would amount to five exabytes. The speed of discovery leaves even our imaginations behind.

So many opportunities, so many cliffs to jump off—a new frontier of ethics, politics, religion and commerce. Centuries of philosophical arguments about free will are now twisted like that DNA strand. Are you truly free to be a size 6 if gluttony is in your genes? The nature-vs.-nurture debate changes when scientists find a gene that makes you shy, makes you reckless, makes you sad. For families haunted by generations of loss to cystic fibrosis and Tay-Sachs disease and sickle-cell anemia, prenatal testing may spare them a future as painful as the past. But if we can screen embryos for curses, should we also screen for gifts? Do you want to know if your child will have perfect pitch or violet eyes? Would parents love their children differently if they designed them to order?

Issues of privacy and knowledge arise every day, particularly as researchers develop tests that spot diseases for which there are no cures. Can it really be kept a secret from your boss or your insurance company or your future spouse that you carry a gene that predicts you will develop Alzheimer's by age 45? Would you want to know that you are likely to develop Huntington's disease if there is still nothing doctors can do to stop it from destroying you?

It is not only our genes we are learning to play with. What if we could create mosquitoes, those flying hypodermics, that instead of spreading malaria spread a vaccine protecting humans against it? Back in 1965, scientists fused mouse and human cells. Today whole animals are being patented; pigs are bred with human cells in hope of finding a source of organ transplants for the 70,000 people on waiting lists in this country alone. And that raises the question: If an Australian biotech company creates a creature that is part human, part pig, what law would apply to it? Should a company be allowed to patent a cloned human embryo, then market its cells to help fight disease? What if the embryo is made of human DNA planted in a cow's egg?

The first insecticide was made from powdered chrysanthemums in China nearly 2,000 years ago. Now biotech companies test bananas that contain a hepatitis vaccine and tomatoes that fight cancer. Dow makes a kind of corn that can turn into biodegradable plastic. Other companies have field-tested a cross between a flounder and a tomato to see if a fish gene can help a fruit stay fresh in freezing weather. The U.S. and the rest of the world are locked in a fight over how much to tinker with and how much to tell about what is now inside what we eat.

If the flip side to all this promise is the challenge that comes with it, perhaps it's a good thing that we may have a long time to weigh the answers. The more scientists learn about the way we age, the more they wonder why we have to. Our skin replaces itself every two weeks, our bones every seven years or so. With the help of the code book, maybe scientists will one day turn our bodies into repair shops, learn how to control the genes that break and those that fix, so that our lives, like

the immortal molecule Watson and Crick deconstructed 50 years ago, go on and on . . .

To say the Human Genome Project was ambitious would be a gross understatement. For more than a decade, scientists from around the globe worked tirelessly to sequence the more than 3 billion DNA letters of the human genome. In 2003, two years ahead of schedule, they proudly proclaimed their success.

As science writer Tim Radford points out in his article "Metaphors and Dreams," understanding our DNA has given us an amazing insight into our own cells, but it hasn't yet told us everything we need to know. Once the Human Genome Project was complete, the National Human Genome Research Institute issued a series of "grand challenges," a sort of large-scale "to do" list for geneticists worldwide.

It may be years before we see a cure—or even more effective treatments—for cancer, Huntington's, or any of the other diseases that afflict humans. But the new set of goals may inspire the scientific community to translate the information gained from the Human Genome Project into new methods to identify diseases before they strike and more powerful tools with which to fight those diseases. —SW

"Metaphors and Dreams: The Paradox of the DNA Revolution Is That It Shows Us a Shining Future Without Telling Us How to Get There"
by Tim Radford
The Scientist, January 13, 2003

The DNA revolution may be just too big to take in: beyond words, even 50 years on. Think of four chemical bases coupled exclusively to each other, adenine with thymine, guanine with cytosine, in a double helix. Then think of this double helix having the power to unwind and duplicate, to make new helixes. So far, so simple. The structure spells out a gene that makes a protein, and makes more DNA.

But like the double helix itself, the challenges divide into questions of scale and complexity. In the nucleus of one cell of one human, tiny braids of DNA twist into two sets of 23 chromosomes. These add up to 3 billion bases, or 200 telephone books of information, or 750,000 pages of typescript, or a procession of nucleotides, which, if read aloud at the rate of one a second, would take almost 100 years to recite. The human body hosts 100 million million cells, and carries the same DNA in almost all of them. Every fragment of this skein of identity was begat by another helix, and every set of chromosomes is descended from two pairs of chromosomes in one single inherited cell.

DNA is not a stable thing. In every cell, the skein is broken and mended, not always correctly, 20,000 times an hour: The joint is jumping, and so is the ligament, and the blood vessel. Much of this DNA is meaningless—human genes are a tiny proportion of the whole—but also unique. Each of the six billion people on the planet carries variants in the genes that make that person different, and lengths of DNA that serve as an identity badge, not just for that person, but also for membership of a family, a clan, a people. So the thread of life links one human to all other people. Forensic scientists use DNA to make family connections: to the bodies of the Romanovs at Ekaterinaburg, to the black slave who bore Thomas Jefferson's children, to the disappeared citizens of Chile and Argentina.

Anthropologists use DNA to trace human lineages: The deeper but still intimate ties between Europeans, Asians, the peoples of the New World and Oceania, all now seem to lead back 100,000 or 200,000 years to a woman in Africa. So DNA makes nonsense of the old idea of race—those notions of purity and separateness so dear to racists—while bewilderingly endorsing the argument that because people inherit propensities to this or that condition, people of different ethnic origins benefit from different medical approaches.

But the thread extends beyond humanity. It ties us to all the other hominids that ever chipped a hand axe, and to all the primates and far beyond, back across hundreds of millions of years to the first creature that crawled gasping from the ancient seas, and far, far beyond that, too, to some last common ancestor in Darwin's warm little pond 3.8 billion years ago. Genes at work in the

Cambrian 550 million years ago are still at work in lawyers, lynxes, and lilacs today.

Memory and Fear

So DNA is all our yesterdays. In the unreadable string of four banal letters is the story of who we are and where we come from. This implies a trajectory, which in turn implies that the journey goes on. Dizzyingly, therefore, our DNA may tell us where we might be going. How much rides on that "may"? What ominous signals lurk in that "might"?

One reaction to these unanswered queries has been an increase in a condition termed biophobia. If DNA is universal, then so is the tissue that it makes. Tinker with the pig insulin gene, and it makes human insulin. Adjust another pig gene, and its heart and lungs and liver start to become compatible with human hearts, lungs, and liver. In the double-helix world, life becomes not some unique, precious property, but a toolkit, a child's Lego set of building blocks, with which to make so many things that nature overlooked: a goat with spider's silk in its milk, a banana that grows vaccines, a mouse with a human ear on its back.

But few embrace the unknown; most of us shrink from it. At its mildest, biophobia is a retreat from laboratory-based science towards the "natural" and the so-called organic: A whole generation clutches the ginkgo biloba bottle instead of the dry martini. At its most dramatic, biophobia has become a batty rejection of science in favor of witchcraft, or the healing power of crystals, or comfrey, or faith itself.

Why be surprised? The biology revolution—Darwin plus DNA—implies that creatures are the sum of their genes plus the selective action of the environment, and that human actions and appetites are rooted in genetics and evolutionary history, just like those of budgerigars, bison, or Mexican jumping beans. Such an empirical history troubles those who think of humankind as separately created by God, as well as those who believe some unique evolutionary advance distinguishes people from their mammalian relatives, so they can confront a higher destiny.

DNA Identity

But how much can our own DNA distinguish us? The code is just that: data, a message. The mysteries deepen within the cell, in which the 30,000 or so genes strung along the DNA switch on and off, in response to some unimaginable cascade of signals, and set up a shuttling of molecules, and a trafficking of energy—an import and export business of nutrients and wastes, to launch a process that ends in a discrete life. The DNA directs a single cell towards a blastocyst, and then an embryo, and then a fetus, and then a baby, and then directs that dainty, moist little being into a sentient, self-aware identity of 100 trillion cells of perhaps 300 specialized kinds.

How does this happen? The DNA doesn't do it; the cell does it. We think of DNA as the software for the cell's computer. That is another analogy we seize upon gratefully, but unhelpfully. The cell itself looks like the leading player in the great game of life. To make sense of the software, we must make sense of the hardware.

To reread James Watson's *The Double Helix* is to see once again the power of the scientific method: Reduce the problem to little solvable bits and attack them serially. The book shares the exhilaration of the discovery of why DNA must be the secret of life.

Metaphor and Mystery

But "must be" is a prediction, not an explanation. The secrets are still there. How could DNA inside the cell make trillions of cells behave as one? What is it about DNA and the cell that makes a protein, that triggers a process, that ends in a firing of electrical signals and discharge of transmitters that assembles a thought, like this one, in these 40 words? What flickering community of a spin doctor's genes set in motion the thought expressed by President Clinton upon the completion of the first drafts of the human genome, on June 26, 2000? He said (and compared to some other things people said, it seemed quite modest), "This is the most important, the most wondrous map ever produced by mankind. It will revolutionize the diagnosis, prevention, and treatment of most, if not all, human diseases." And could there have been a genetic basis for the response of 100,000 clinicians, biomedical researchers, health managers, and patients: "Yes, but how? And when?"

Encouraging initiatives have emerged from the decade that ended in Clinton's hyperbole. A group of boys in the United Kingdom and France born with X-linked severe combined immune deficiency have begun to lead almost normal lives, although one has now developed leukemia. Gene-based medicine has yet to help a child with cystic fibrosis, or an adult with Huntington disease, or patients with more than a handful of the so-called single-gene disorders. Yet therapies for these conditions were supposed to be the foothills of gene-based medicine. The big challenges, everybody said, lay in the complexity of cardiovascular afflictions and cancers.

Right now, more than half of all gene-based therapy trials are aimed at cancer, and the juries could be out a long time. Treatment to extend life will, by definition, take at least a lifetime to validate. The paradox of the DNA revolution is that it shows us a shining future without telling us how to get there.

It will be a long time before gene-based medicine cures diabetes, stops migraine, or reverses neurodegeneration. It may never do these things. But if you have the complete maker's manual for the pathogen that gives you malaria, tuberculosis, or flu, and if you also have the complete instruction kit for the assembly not just of any human, but the one with the infection, then you ought to be able to think of a treatment.

In the 18th Century, doctors prescribed medicines—arsenic, sulfur, that sort of thing—with no idea of whether they would work. In the 20th century, doctors discovered medicines that would sometimes work, but the physicians didn't know why. Tomorrow's doctors will understand exactly why some infections kill, and how they can be circumvented. Once doctors were valued for their bedside manners. Some future generation of medics may cure illnesses even without seeing the patient.

Tomorrow's Science

But the great leap forward will not simply be in more—and more expensive—medicines. At some point in the future, people studying the genetic data and the survival of patients will also begin to understand how the immune system really works. If they can understand that, then perhaps they can help people not to fall ill in the first place.

There will be a much greater understanding of the link between diet and health. Akin to the ginkgo biloba approach, this time, the recipe for health will be based on true biochemistry. If antioxidants in red wine, rhubarb, or rice pudding really do protect the heart and demolish tumor cells, then they will be enthusiastically cultivated. The phrase, "a hearty meal," will take on new meaning. And then seamlessly from the chef's fork to the surgeon's knife, surgery will continue to become more precise and more effective, and recovery less painful.

But the same intricate knowledge of how cells act and interact is already pointing to other things: tissue engineering, for instance. Researchers now grow human skin. One day, someone could be injecting you with cultured versions of your own brain cells. Phrases like "fresh thinking" will also take on a new meaning.

We have embarked on the second information revolution; we are about to know ourselves in a way that was once unimaginable. Maybe we really are blinded by science. It could be that we have opened a door into a future so brilliant that all we can do is blink, until our eyes adjust. And maybe—with bioterrorism, ecodestruction, gross economic inequality, or just old-fashioned hubris—we will increase the scale of human suffering in the course of trying to alleviate it.

No ordinary, prescriptive language can encompass the DNA revolution; for the moment, it is beyond words. This is why scientists and fundraisers and journalists alike fall back upon metaphors. But metaphors can mislead. It might be fair, however, to compare the DNA revolution with the Promethean theft of fire from heaven. Fire is a source of light, and part of alchemy's tool-kit. It enables life and threatens it, too. Of course we will burn our fingers. But who now could imagine life without fire?

In "The Human Genome Project: The Next Decade," pediatric professor R. M. Gardiner follows the Human Genome Project from its launch in 1990 to the release of the complete draft of the human genome in 2001. He shows how scientists have identified the total number of human genes and their functions, mapped the architecture of the human genome and chromosomes, and gained the ability to compare and contrast the human genome with those of other organisms (such as yeast and the fruit fly Drosophila).

Since the article was written, scientists have completed the human genome sequence. But they are still working, as Gardiner points out, to understand the full extent of genetic variation and to comprehend fully the genetic basis of diseases with complex inheritance patterns by analyzing changes to single nucleotides, called single nucleotide polymorphisms, or SNPs.

Researchers have also completed sequencing of the mouse genome, and for the first time they have been able to compare what they know of our genome with that of another mammal. They have discovered that mice and humans have a strikingly similar number of genes (from 20,000 to 25,000), and that more than 90 percent of the mouse genome lines up with a region on our own genome. The other significant sequencing project mentioned in this article—that of the zebrafish—was begun in 2001 and is expected to be completed by the end of 2005. —SW

"The Human Genome Project: The Next Decade"
by R. M. Gardiner
Archives of Disease in Childhood, June 1, 2002

A draft version of the complete human genome sequence was published early in 2001. This was the culmination of both public and privately funded efforts initiated a decade ago. The new landscape of the genome contained several surprises, including the relatively small number of genes, 30–40,000, required to make a human. Attention has now shifted towards annotating the genome by assigning function to all the genes, and characterising human genetic variation manifested as single nucleotide polymorphisms (SNPs). The latter should allow the genetic basis of common disorders with "complex" inheritance to be elucidated.

Ten years ago I wrote a review for this journal entitled "The human genome: a prospect for paediatrics."[1] In doing so a well known Goldwynism was ignored: "Never make predictions, especially about the future." From today's perspective the predictions in that article seem, however, rather cautious. The major goals of the Human Genome Project (HGP) which had just been initiated have been attained ahead of schedule and the molecular genetic analysis of rare human diseases continues to generate new biological insights of extraordinary depth. Yet for the paediatrician dealing with the daily round of childhood diseases the impact remains negligible, and it is true that our present knowledge of the human genome resembles a gigantic "parts" list in which at least half of the items have a catalogue number but no assigned function. So how has this project progressed so fast, where do we stand now, and what of the next one or two decades?

The Human Genome Project (HGP): The Past 10 Years

The HGP was launched in September 1990 with a projected completion date of 2005. The idea that sequencing the entire human genome might be a worthwhile endeavour arose in the mid 1980s, about a decade after Frederick Sanger and others introduced methods for sequencing DNA. This proposal sparked a fierce debate. Critics argued that it would be a mindless factory project siphoning research funds away from hypothesis driven research, that most of the sequence was "junk" of little biological interest, and that the sheer size of the human genome precluded its completion within a reasonable time frame without entirely new methodology.

The project was launched despite opposition and most of these fears have proved unfounded. Although completion of the sequence remained the ultimate goal, the project always encompassed wider aims and the creation of genetic and physical maps represented an essential preliminary to large scale sequencing. Most importantly it also included the sequencing of several model organisms and funding for the development of bioinformatics and research on the ethical, legal, and social implications of the project.

Genomes of increasing size and complexity were completed in rapid succession. The first genome of a living organism, *Haemophilus influenzae*, was sequenced in 1995, and those of baker's yeast (*Saccharomyces cerevisiae*), the round worm (*Caenorhabditis elegans*), fruit fly (*Drosophila melanogaster*), and mustard weed (*Arabidopsis thaliana*) followed in rapid succession between 1996 and 2000. The last three of these have genomes of around 100 million base pairs, roughly equivalent to that of a medium sized human chromosome and just one thirtieth of the size of the entire human genome. Sequences of the two smallest human chromosomes were published in late 1999 and of course the complete "draft" of the human genome early in 2001. Competition between private and public sequencing efforts generated acrimony but spurred progress, and was a factor in the sequence being completed ahead of schedule.

The Landscape of the Human Genome

The papers published simultaneously in two leading scientific journals[2, 3] represent a milestone in biology and provided some fascinating new insights into the genetic blueprint of man. In this brief review, there is space to consider three of these: the architecture of the genome, the total number of human genes and their functions, and the comparisons which are now possible between human genes and those of other fully sequenced organisms.

Genome Architecture: Freeloaders and Fossils

It was already known that protein coding sequences accounted for just 1.5 % of the genome and that introns accounted for a further 24 %. It is now clear that an unprecedented proportion, more than half, of the human eukaryotic genome consists of repeat sequences, the majority of which are so called transposable elements or transposons. It seems likely that most of these repeats are simply parasitic, selfish DNA elements, "freeloaders" that use the genome as a convenient host.

Moreover, in humans most of these parasitic DNA repeats are very ancient and enfeebled. By contrast, the mouse genome has younger, actively reinserting sequences but they comprise a much smaller fraction of the genome. Is the human genome just lackadaisical about cleaning out these relics or do they serve some useful purpose? There is evidence that repeat sequences may have some positive effects, for example, in shaping the evolution of the genome and in creating new genes.

Chromosomal Architecture: Variation in Gene Density and Transcriptional Activity

It is now possible to generate a provisional "human transcriptome map" which reveals the gene expression profiles for any chromosomal region in various tissue types. This shows a striking tendency of highly expressed genes to cluster in specific chromosomal regions of high gene density. It is also apparent that whole chromosomes may differ in these respects. Chromosome 19 is packed with genes at an average of 23 per megabase, whereas chromosome 13 is gene poor at just five genes per megabase. Interestingly the three chromosomes responsible for most constitutional trisomies, 13, 18, and 21 all show low gene density and low gene expression. Presumably this accounts for the non-lethal effects of an extra copy of these chromosomes.

Gene Number: Not So Many

The total number of human genes remains uncertain, but has been revised downwards from upper estimates of 150,000 to 30–40,000. Should this be regarded as a blow to our speciocentric view of the biological world? This number of coding genes compares with 6,000 for yeast, 13,000 for the fruit fly, 18,000 for the round worm, and 26,000 for a humble plant, the mustard weed.

It seems likely that the number will be revised upwards. Finding human genes is a difficult task, even with sequence in hand. Methods for gene prediction depend on looking for signatures of gene structure such as open reading frames, homologies to sequences of human genes, and evidence that a DNA sequence is expressed as messenger RNA. Long introns and rare transcripts make some genes difficult to detect and these may comprise the so called "dark matter" of undiscovered genes.

However, it is clear that the relation between gene number and biological complexity is not linear and the n value paradox may be more apparent than real. For example, taking a trivial mathematical model of biological complexity in which complexity is defined as the number of possible transcriptome states and a gene is either ON or OFF, a genome with n genes can encode 2^n states. On this basis, an extra 10,000 genes provides $2^{10,000}$ extra states, a vast number, which certainly allows human beings to consider themselves superior to worms.

Gene Complement and Structure

It is also now possible to compare the nature and structure of human genes with those of other organisms with sequenced genomes. It is clear that most of our genes come from the distant evolutionary past. Genes involved in basic cellular functions, such as DNA replication and transcription, have evolved only once and remained fixed. Only about 10% of the protein families in our genome are specific to vertebrates. Human proteins are built from more domains and new combinations of domains, new architectures using old bricks. However, certain gene families do appear to have expanded in vertebrates. Some subs serve vertebrate specific functions such as blood clotting or the acquired immune response. Others provide increased general capabilities such as genes for signalling, apoptosis, or control of gene transcription. The human genome is particularly rich in Zinc finger genes.

It is also clear that individual human genes encode a much wider repertoire of proteins, on average three or four, by mechanisms such as alternative splicing.

Future Prospects

If we fast forward to 2010, or even 2020, what changes can we expect in biology and medicine of special relevance to paediatricians? In the field of genomics the immediate challenges include completion of the human genome sequence, annotation of the genome, and characterisation of the pattern and extent of human genetic variation. At the present time the genomes of about three dozen organisms, most of those single cell microbes, have been completely sequenced. Model organisms next in line for complete sequencing include the mouse and zebrafish, and by 2020 it is anticipated that 1000 complete genomes will be in hand. In parallel however, interest is inevitably shifting already from genomics to proteomics.

In paediatrics the dissection of the molecular basis of rare Mendelian and chromosomal disorders will continue apace. More important perhaps, for the general paediatrician, is the prospect of understanding common early onset disorders with "complex" inheritance. These include asthma, type 1 diabetes mellitus, and the epilepsies, but also surgical abnormalities such as cleft lip and palate and pyloric stenosis, and the behavioural phenotypes of autism and attention deficit hyperactivity disorder. Of course, the leap from understanding to effective intervention is even more difficult, but at least a start will have been made. A selection of these themes are considered in more detail.

The Human Genome: Annotation and Characterising Variation

So called annotation of the human genome remains a huge task. Not only must all the genes be identified, but functions must be assigned to the proteins they encode. As the final sequence is assembled the computer programs used to predict the presence of a gene will come closer to identifying a complete inventory, but their inherent limitations render this a difficult task as positional cloners searching through large genomic regions harbouring a disease gene already known.

Preliminary analysis of the predicted human protein coding genes has allowed functions to be tentatively assigned to about 50% of the putative gene products. Of

26,588 predicted human proteins, the most common molecular functions are transcription factors (1850, 6%) and nucleic acid enzymes (2308, 7.5%). Other highly represented functions include receptors, kinases, and hydrolases. There are 406 ion channels and 533 transporters. But there are 12,809 predicted proteins of unknown function. Some of these may represent false positive gene predictions but the rest remind us of how much remains to be discovered about the basic biology of man.

The second great task is the detailed characterisation of human genetic variation. On average, the genomes of two human individuals are 99.9% identical. The 0.1% which differs is what makes us individuals rather than clones. Most of the variation is represented by alterations at single nucleotides. A single nucleotide polymorphism, or SNP (pronounced SNiP), is defined as a single base pair in genomic DNA at which different alleles (bases) exist in normal individuals in some populations, with the minor allele frequency greater than 1%. The SNPs are likely to include the allelic variation that accounts for common disease traits (see below).

A massive effort is now in progress to characterise human genetic variation and create a SNP map of the human genome. A particular SNP may or may not influence the phenotype, depending on its nature and location. For example, a SNP in a coding region (cSNP) may alter an amino acid and a SNP in a regulatory region may alter gene expression. Most SNPs are however in introns or intergenic regions and are assumed to be "neutral" in evolutionary terms. Identified SNPs are then used to create "haplotype" maps which reflect the phenomenon of linkage disequilibrium (LD). LD is the non-random occurrence of specific alleles at adjacent loci. When a base change first occurs it does so on a particular chromosome with particular haplotypes-pattern of alleles at adjacent SNPs. Over time, meiotic recombination and other factors erode the haplotypes until linkage equilibrium, or random association is established.

The extent and pattern of LD within the human genome and across human genes is just beginning to emerge.[4] Empirical data indicate that extensive blocks of LD are present, at least in the Northern European population, which create haplotypes between 25 and 100 Kb in length. This is good news for the analysis of "complex" disease (see below) and probably reflects a recent bottleneck in human evolutionary history. Moreover, it appears likely that it will be possible to identify a small number of SNPs, perhaps half a dozen, in the average human gene, which will allow the main haplotypes of that gene present in a given population to be determined.

Model Organisms: Mouse and Zebrafish

At the top of the list of model organism genomes to be sequenced comes the humble mouse. This small, furry creature shared a last common ancestor with humans about 100 million years ago. Its genome is similar in size to the human and the gene complement is similar. A host of human disease genes have orthologues in

[the] mouse, and identification of genes causing many of the many naturally occurring mutant phenotypes known has often helped in isolation of the corresponding human disease gene. Many extended chromosomal regions have maintained the same genes in the same order, so called conserved synteny.

Two new developments will build on the mouse genome sequence. Mutagenesis screens are under-way to mutate many more mouse genes as a powerful strategy for assigning function. Secondly, it is likely that mouse models will prove extremely useful for unravelling the causes of disorders with "complex" inheritance.

Next in line is a small tropical fish, the zebrafish *Danio reria* which separated from humans 400 million years ago and promises to serve as the "canonical" vertebrate, especially for the investigation of development. It is the first vertebrate to prove tractable to large scale genetic screening of the kind used so successfully in fruit flies and worms. Developmental phenotypes are readily observed, thanks to its external development and transparency. Developmental programmes are highly conserved among vertebrates, and mutations in orthologous zebrafish genes have already provided models for human genetic disorders such as porphyria and Usher 1B syndrome. Like the mouse, large regions of human and zebrafish chromosomes show conserved synteny.

Analysis of Disorders with "Complex" Inheritance

A number of common, important childhood onset diseases display familial clustering which is best explained by so called multifactorial inheritance: an interplay between several genes and environmental factors. These include type 1 diabetes mellitus, asthma, inflammatory bowel disease, the epilepsies, obesity, and behavioural disorders such as attention deficit hyperactivity disorder and autism.

In the past decade the spectacular successes seen in isolation of the genes for Mendelian diseases has not been matched by success in identification of susceptibility genes for disorders with such so called "complex inheritance." In fact numerous genome wide linkage studies have frustratingly failed to find clear and replicable evidence for the location of the genes responsible for these traits. In any event, where good evidence for linkage has been found, the chromosomal region implicated has been extremely large.

Optimists believe this is about to change following the generation of so called SNP maps which can be used to find susceptibility loci by means of association rather than linkage. In reality success will depend on certain features of both the nature of human genetic variation and the genetic architecture of these common diseases.[5] As described above, recent data indicate that "blocks" of LD in the human genome are larger than some theoretical considerations had predicted. This means that genome wide searches can use fewer SNPs, although it creates a potential difficulty that if several sequence variants are inherited together (that is, are in LD) it will be less easy to spot the causal variant. Moreover, it appears that common variants of most genes can be characterised by a small number of SNP haplotypes, facilitating candidate gene association studies.

Of equal importance however, is the true genetic architecture of "complex" traits. A spectrum of possibilities exists concerning the number of loci, the magnitude of their individual effect on risk, their mode of interaction, and the number and population frequency of disease susceptibility alleles. The latter is particularly important. The so called "common disease-common variant" hypothesis suggests that each locus will harbour only a few susceptibility alleles, each at high frequency (for example, >5–10%) in the population. Recent calculations suggest that this will be the case,[6] but if it is not, association studies are doomed to failure. A large number of rare (<1%) alleles would be very difficult to detect using association analysis.

A recent application of the strategy of linkage analysis followed by association studies has resulted in the identification of a gene for Crohn's disease, NOD2 in the pericentromic region of chromosome 16p.[7,8] If the underlying biology is favourable, this could be the first of many susceptibility genes for common diseases isolated during the next decade.

Conclusion

In the 1990 article I concluded that "the human genome today is as much a dark continent as Africa in the early nineteenth century. Its exploration is about to begin." Phase 1 of that exploration has now been completed, but much of the excitement and exploitation remains in the future.

References

1. Gardiner RM. The human genome: a prospect for paediatrics. *Arch Dis Child* 1990;65:457–61.

2. The human genome. *Nature* 2001;409:813–958.

3. The human genome. *Science* 2001;291:1145–1434.

4. Daly MJ, Rioux JD, Schaffner SF, *et al*. High-resolution haplotypes structure in the human genome. *Nat Genet* 2001;29:229–32.

5. Wright AF, Hastie ND. Complex genetic diseases: controversy over the Croesus code. *Genome Biology* 2001;2:2007.1–2007.8.

6. Reich DE, Lander ES. On the allelic spectrum of human disease. *Trends Genet* 2001;17:502–10.

7. Ogura Y, Bonen DK, Inohara N, *et al*. A frameshift mutation in NOD2 associated with susceptibility to Crohn's disease. *Nature* 2001;411:603–6.

8. Hugot J-P, Chamaillard M, Zouali H, *et al*. Association of NOD2 leucine-rich repeat variants with susceptibility to Crohn's disease. *Nature* 2001;411:599–603.

Archives of Disease in Childhood, June 1, 2002. Vol. 86. Reprinted with permission from the BMJ Publishing Group.

In the early 1900s, biologist Thomas Hunt Morgan (1866–1945) was conducting research in the Zoology Department at Columbia University in New York. Gregor Mendel's breeding experiments and theories of heredity had just been rediscovered by the scientific community, but Morgan wanted to take them one step further. He wanted to uncover the genetic basis for heredity—to know exactly what those "traits" that Mendel had described were and where they were located.

Morgan chose for his research the fly Drosophila melanogaster because it was cheap, easy to breed in the laboratory, and it had a readily observable short life cycle. He bred the flies, looking for mutations—observable changes in the fly's body. His experiments finally yielded a fly with white eyes, rather than the normal red. He discovered that only male flies were born with this mutation. Morgan's research led him to the hypothesis that eye color follows a sex-linked inheritance. Even more important, he introduced the ideas that chromosomes contain certain genes and that genes exist in specific locations along the chromosome. It was a major break-through in the study of genetics.

A century later, scientists are still busy studying the Drosophila *for the clues it can provide us about our genes. Of course, scientists have now sequenced the entire* Drosophila *genome to reveal its more than 13,000 genes. They have also sequenced the nematode worm, mouse, and yeast, and are working on several other model organisms that should give even greater insight into our genetic makeup. Freelance writer Douglas Steinberg introduces us to the "illuminating behaviors" that have helped scientists learn about evolutionary behaviors in general. —SW*

"Illuminating Behaviors"
by Douglas Steinberg
The Scientist, June 2, 2003

If not for Nobel laureates Thomas Hunt Morgan, Eric R. Kandel, and Sydney Brenner, the notion of a general behavioral model might seem odd. Behaviors, after all, are determined by an animal's evolutionary history and ecological niche. They are often idiosyncratic, shared in detail only by closely related species.

But, thanks to Morgan's research in the early 20th century, and Kandel's and Brenner's work over the past 35 years, the fly *Drosophila melanogaster*, the mollusk *Aplysia californica*, and the worm *Caenorhabditis elegans* have become general behavioral models. The newest member of the club is the mouse.

This quartet yields broadly applicable behavioral findings for two reasons: First, these animals are unusually amenable to cellular and molecular experimentation; second, such experimentation has turned up certain genes, proteins, and cells that underlie behavior across many species. Evolution did not "completely reinvent the wheel and come up with a new set of molecular rules for each phylum," notes *Aplysia* expert Thomas J. Carew, at the University of California, Irvine.

Learning from Sea Slugs

Lacking a cortex, *Aplysia* has just 20,000 neurons clustered into ganglia. As such, its nervous system appears incommensurable with those of higher organisms. But this hand-length, maroon sea slug has one quality trumping interspecies differences: huge neurons, many with cell bodies hundreds of microns across. Biologists can easily image and manipulate these neurons to determine their firing properties and responses to stimulation. Popular research areas include the mollusk's feeding behavior and its withdrawal reflexes when it is touched.

One important discovery, says Carew, is that facilitation—a phenomenon involving enhanced neurotransmitter release into the synapses separating neurons—underlies a simple form of learning known as sensitization. Other findings have elucidated the signal-transduction pathways triggered by learning. Cyclic AMP (cAMP) activates cytoplasmic kinases (e.g., protein kinase A), which translocate to the nucleus where they activate transcription factors (e.g., cAMP response element-binding protein). These factors then turn on genes whose protein products cause long-term changes in the neuron.

Many findings in *Aplysia* have been replicated in *Drosophila* and mice. Experiments on transgenic and knockout mice, for example, show that synaptic plasticity relies on several kinases and transcription factors first explored in *Aplysia*. Conversely, knowledge gleaned from higher organisms might apply to sea slugs. Using a paradigm tested in humans, Carew learned that training the mollusk induces long-term memory if sessions are separated in time but not if they are massed together.

Aplysia has two major limitations as a model for higher organisms: a modest behavioral repertoire, and a genome that has not been sequenced (unlike the genomes of the other three behavioral models). To manipulate this mollusk genetically, researchers inject mRNA directly into its neurons.

Lords of the Flies

Genetic plasticity is *Drosophila*'s chief advantage. In 1915, the Columbia lab of fruit-fly pioneer Morgan conducted the first behavioral genetics study of any organism, recounts Brandeis University biologist Jeffrey C. Hall. Since then, scientists have discovered or created thousands of fly mutants. Tools for investigating *Drosophila* include heat-inducible and tetracycline-regulated transgenes, transposable P-elements, and the GAL4-UAS system, which allows precise spatial control of transgene expression.

Many fly researchers are examining circadian cycling between activity and inactivity, as well as learning and memory.[1] Some are focusing on courtship, geotaxis, and reactions to odor and taste. At least 15 homologs of fly genes implicated in these behaviors have been found in other species, Hall says.

Drosophila learning occurs during natural behaviors—courtship, for example, is not totally hard-wired—and in conditioning experiments. Martin Heisenberg, at the University of Würzburg in Germany, has trained flies to avoid the heated side of a chamber and devised a complex flight simulator to test visual learning. One popular type of apparatus shocks flies as they sniff an odor. Some mutant or transgenic flies later forget to avoid the odor.

Neuroscientist Jerry C. P. Yin, at Cold Spring Harbor Laboratory, learned that one murine transgene actually enhances certain forms of *Drosophila* memory.

It encodes a specific form of the signal-transduction enzyme protein kinase C. Based on this protein's functions in other cell types and species, Yin speculates that it allows a neuron to tag its recently active synapses.

Two other Cold Spring Harbor neuroscientists, Tim Tully and Josh Dubnau, used the odor/shock assay to uncover about 60 putative memory genes. Switching to DNA chip technology, Tully and Dubnau identified 42 genes that turn on or off during memory formation. Prominent among the genes implicated by both methods were *staufen*, whose protein product appears to be involved in transporting mRNAs to synapses, and *pumilio*, whose product seems to help repress translation during mRNA transport.

Hall specializes in the *fruitless* gene, which encodes a transcription factor critical to male courtship. He regards *fruitless* as the best example of a single gene specifying a set of behaviors. His lab found that *fruitless* is expressed throughout the fly's nervous system—a discovery, he notes, that is consistent with the gene's broad effects.

Genetic malleability, *Drosophila*'s greatest strength, also can be a weakness. In rapidly breeding mutant populations, further mutations often cause loss of phenotype, which is difficult to reverse. (Labs cannot preserve the original phenotype because there are no reliable methods to freeze and thaw fly embryos.) For neurobiologists, the fly's main drawback is that its 150,000 or so neurons are too small to manipulate in situ, except at the neuromuscular junction.

Nothing to Hide

The nematode *C. elegans* joined the behavioral-model menagerie basically because it has nothing to hide. The tiny transparent worm's nervous system has been completely plotted, revealing 302 neurons and 5000 synapses. With this knowledge in hand, researchers employ various cell-ablation and gene-manipulation techniques to link behaviors to specific cells and genes. Investigators also can record from nematode neurons and recently began culturing them.

Worms have a limited behavioral repertoire. Besides life- and species-preserving activities such as feeding, mating, and egg-laying, nematodes "can't do much—swim forward, swim backward, stop, start, curl in a circle," observes psychology professor Catherine H. Rankin, at the University of British Columbia.[2] Nevertheless, their exquisite sensitivities to temperature and ambient chemicals facilitate behavioral conditioning experiments. Homologs of *Drosophila* learning-associated genes are known, but their effects on *C. elegans* learning are unclear, says Rankin. Altering these signal-transduction genes, she explains, often results in an uncoordinated worm, a common and unrevealing mutant phenotype.

Even when a mutation's impact seems unambiguous, the full story is probably far from simple. Five years ago, neuroscientists Mario de Bono, now at the Medical Research Council's Laboratory of Molecular Biology in Cambridge, England, and Cornelia I. Bargmann at UC-San Francisco, discovered a loss-of-function mutation in a receptor gene that switched *C. elegans* from a solitary food-forager to a "social" one that gathers with its mates on their common source of nourishment, a lawn of bacteria.

Follow-up work suggests the existence of "multiple layers of antagonistic stimuli that are regulating whether you are social or solitary," says de Bono. "There's often this assumption that because a single gene flips behavior from one form to another, it is the critical gene." But, he demurs: "You can still have that effect when you have a gene that's only one player in a larger number of players."

Knockouts and Their Discontents

Rats were long the rodent behavioral model of choice because of their intelligence and large brains. Over the past decade, however, transgenic mice have increasingly hogged the spotlight. (Transgenic rats are relatively rare, because foreign DNA does not incorporate readily into the genomic DNA of rat oocytes, explains Markus Heilig, at the Karolinska Institute, Sweden.) Jacqueline N. Crawley, chief of the National Institute of Mental Health's behavioral genomics section, notes that transgenic mice have become invaluable in experiments involving learning and memory, motor disorders such as Parkinson disease, and obesity.[3]

Mice lacking certain genes can display complex behavioral phenotypes, such as social deficits (knockout of the hormone oxytocin); less huddling and nest-building (knockout of the intracellular signaling molecule dishevelled-1); and male aggression (knockout of neuronal nitric oxide synthase). But Crawley cautions that different murine strains with an identical genetic alteration might each exhibit a unique phenotype. The likely reason: Each strain harbors a different set of polymorphisms that temper the genetic alteration's effect.

Transgenic studies involve other complexities and pitfalls. Crawley observes, for example, that some murine wild-type strains are already so aggressive that an aggression-causing mutation might be undetectable. She also warns of "a lot of variability in behavior that requires larger numbers of animals and more rigorous statistics than molecular geneticists are used to." When these requirements are not met, she adds, investigators often overinterpret results, causing the field of behavioral neuroscience to lose some credibility.

Crawley's mantra is that "behavior is not so simple." But that's a challenge that *Drosophila* expert Hall relishes. He insists that biologists "should want the phenomenon [they study] to be complicated, because life is complicated."

References

1. M. B. Sokolowski, "*Drosophila*: Genetics meets behaviour," *Nat Rev Genet*, 2:879-90, 2001.

2. C. H. Rankin, "From gene to identified neuron to behaviour in *Caenorhabditis elegans*," *Nat Rev Genet*, 3:622-30, 2002.

3. J. N. Crawley, *What's Wrong With My Mouse? Behavioral Phenotyping of Transgenic and Knockout Mice*, New York: John Wiley & Sons, 2000.

The title of this chapter is "What Can Our DNA Tell Us About Ourselves?" Bioinformatics is not the what—it is the how. As scientists of the Human Genome Project sift through the more than 3 billion chemical bases that make up the human genome, they are generating a massive amount of data. Sophisticated computer databases are needed to store, organize, retrieve, and analyze that data. The merging of biological science and computer technology has given rise to the new discipline of bioinformatics.

In his article, industry analyst Giridhar Rao discusses the sophisticated technology needed to translate billions of units of genetic code into workable data that scientists can use to develop new disease treatments. He shows how data must be translated into code that computers can understand. And he illustrates just how much storage capacity is needed to hold the massive amounts of data contained in the entire human genome. —SW

"Bioinformatics—New Horizons, New Hopes"
by Giridhar Rao
Drug Discovery & Development, July 1, 2004

Bioinformatics, in terms of technology and business value propositions, has been growing at a rapid pace over the last five years but is still considered an emerging market. Hwa Lim, president of D'Trends Inc., of San Ramon, Calif., coined the term "bioinformatics" in a journal article in 1987, based on the concept of biological information being stored and transferred by DNA.

However, bioinformatics as a field existed even before it was named. Pauling's theory of molecular evolution (1962) is considered to have flagged off this field. Margaret Oakley Dayhoff is said to be the pioneering founder of this field and with her work—*Atlas of Protein Sequence and Structure* (1965)—became the first person to use computers in chemistry and biology.

Over the years, market trends have dictated the growth of bioinformatics-affecting companies such as Double Twist of Oakland, Calif., which folded in 2002. Celera Genomics, Rockville, Md., and Incyte Corp., Wilmington, De., leaders in the field, had to change over from pure informatics-based approaches to applied approaches to survive.

There are many different definitions and explanations to "what is bioinformatics?" In simple terms, it is a multidisciplinary and scientific approach that depends foremost on the application of information technology to the biological sciences. In a classical sense, bioinformatics enables the utilization of advanced computer science technology to understand and integrate molecular biology and genetics—particularly to comprehend the maze of the complex structures and functions of the individual components of a living cell with respect to the well being of the entire organism.

Our Cellular Map

It took 13 years, $250 million, and more than 1,100 biologists, computer scientists, and technicians working in six countries to decipher 3.1 billion chemical "letters" of the human genome. Finally, the human genetic code was mapped in 2000, which is the single most important event to stimulate a surge in research and development activities in many fields related to biology and healthcare. The bioinformatics sector is set to gain immense benefits from this monumental work.

However, the completion of the human genome project is just scratching the tip of the iceberg. An estimated 40,000 genes in Homo sapiens have been characterized in the completed draft of the human genome. There are around 200 proteins per gene and, to compound the complexity, there exist modifications to more than 100 known biochemical post-translational proteins. The number of proteins that still need to be identified could be as high as eight million or more. As a whole, these diverse types of data have created a huge challenge for drug discovery researchers to obtain promising targets.

We are moving into an era where drugs may be designed as per individual genetic profiles. Bioinformatics is now proving to be a powerful tool in the battle against toxicity and last-stage drug failures. The pharmaceuticals industry is the biggest beneficiary of the bioinformatics revolution. Pharmaceutical companies could potentially save several years of research in new drug design and introduction, and many millions of dollars, by integrating data and information across disciplines, pharmaceuticals departments, processes, and drugs.

The "isms" of the "ics"

Bioinformatics stands at the crossroads of multiple domains linking genomics, proteomics, and transcriptional data with medicinal pharmacology, amongst others. In this era of "ics," bioinformatics endows essential information about the functional analysis of genes, including genetic variation and multigenic diseases.

As computing and biology have converged, software tools for data capture, management, analysis, mining, and dissemination have emerged. Additionally, hardware that helps in precise data generation in the life sciences is on the rise. Multiple sources of biological and chemical data are being harnessed by genomics or gene-sequencing projects, high-throughput screening, combinatorial chemical synthesis, gene-expression investigations, pharmacogenomics, and proteomics studies, creating explosive volumes of data. The data thus generated poses a challenge in itself to drug discovery and development. Relating and turning this complexity of data into useful information and knowledge is the primary goal of bioinformatics.

Running through genetic variations and the incredible task of deciphering proteins is virtually impossible without Information Technology (IT). Hardware companies provide equipment to handle the vast quantities of data. Software tools capture, manage, and analyze that data. Pharmaceutical and biotech companies need IT infrastructure to do meaningful research. High-profile companies such as IBM, Motorola Inc., Compaq Computer Corp., and Sun Microsystems Inc., have set up life sciences divisions and have invested in bioinformatics companies to gain a foothold in this sector. Myriad Genetics Inc., Salt Lake City, Utah, best known for discovering the gene linked to hereditary breast cancer, formed a $185 million joint venture with Oracle (the world's largest software company) and Hitachi (Japan's largest electronics major) in April 2001. The venture will compile information gleaned on proteins and their interactions with human cells and create a proprietary database by 2004. Similarly, the Celera Genomics group, which completed the mapping of the human genome in 2000, has tied up with Compaq and the US Department of Energy's Sandia National Laboratory.

Evolution of IT

One of the common tasks being performed via bioinformatics is comparing sequence data. This procedure of comparing sequences can involve various similarity searches, including homology and motif searches. While homology searches compare whole sequences, motif searches look at localized sections and their associated functions. Similarly, a protein sequence can be compared to DNA databases, or vice-versa.

Major companies offering sequence data include Celera and Incyte. GenBank at the National Center for Biotechnology Information, the DNA Data Bank of Japan, and the European Molecular Biology Laboratory database are the main public sources for DNA sequences. The Protein Information Resource International Protein Sequence Database and SWISS-PROT are the primary public sources for amino acid sequences. Several other focused sequence databases exist, some specializing in particular species and others specializing in particular data types, such as tRNA. There are various algorithms to choose from for performing searches. Many of these are fast and approximate while others are slower and more computationally aggressive. Examples of these algorithms include SmithWaterman, BLAST, and FASTA. Dynamic programming, neural networks, and other methods are also widely used.

Leading the technology companies in meeting the daunting demand of computational analysis, is the computer giant IBM Corp., Armonk, N.Y. Apart from a host of biotech-related work, IBM has invested $100 million to build Blue Gene, a superfast computer exclusively meant for bioinformatics. It has also invested an initial $100 million in developing IT to help organize and interpret genetic code. Through its Life Sciences division, IBM has entered into a partnership with Incyte Genomics Inc. IBM's Discovery Link data management software will organize the biotech firm's large amount of genomic information contained in its Genomic Knowledge Platform.

Other IT majors such as Oracle, Sun Microsystems, Motorola, Compaq, Microsoft, Silicon Graphics (SGI), and Corning are vying to catch up with IBM. Microsoft offers built-in data-mining tools for picking out important information from a large database, which forms the crux of genetic research. Celera Genomics chose Compaq as its IT partner to develop the world's largest genomics computing and sequencing facility. It equipped Celera with more than 900 high-performance Alpha processors and Compaq Storage-Works to manage what is today a 100-terabyte database. Oracle's 9i is the database of choice for life sciences companies in the data management and database segment. Motorola exploits the biotech opportunities in biochips, while SGI has a sequence-comparison application called Blast.

IBM was the first to build the world's most powerful computing grid for life sciences. It is known as the Distributed Terascale Facility (DTF), to enable thousands of scientists around the United States to share computing resources over the world's fastest research network. DTF's interconnected Linux clusters will be capable of 13.6 trillion calculations per second with a storage capacity of more than 600 terabytes of data.

ACGT to 01 101 10 . . . do we understand enough? Most biological processes are basically governed by the genetic codes: DNAs and RNAs. These molecules are composed of a string of four chemical "letters" called adenine, cytosine, guanine, and thymine, normally abbreviated to A, C, G, and T, respectively. However, in a computed problem solving and data analysis environment, a code of different order—digital code—exists. In digital data memory, storage, processing, and communications, values of 0 and 1 are utilized in the algorithms.

Central to the field of bioinformatics is the problem of expression, i.e., to express the problem in such a way or in the correct dimension so that computers can understand. High-performance computing and communication technologies are in use for biological information management. However, much still needs to be achieved to bridge the gap between the two universal codes essential to bioinformatics.

IT companies will be required to design tools and develop R&D and product strategies to capture DNA sequencing data from both the Human Genome Project (HGP) and individual samples, as well as to analyze and create information as required by researchers.

Decoding Complexity

The human genome's structure is extraordinarily complex and its function is poorly understood. Only 1% to 2% of its bases, encode proteins, and the full complement of protein-coding sequences still remains to be established. About as much of the non-coding portion is probably functionally important, too, but little is known about it. The hunch is that it contains the bulk of the regulatory information controlling the expression of the protein-coding genes, along with other functions such as non-protein-coding genes and the sequence determinants of chromosome dynamics.

Comparing genome sequences from evolutionarily diverse species is a powerful tool for identifying functionally important genomic elements. Essentially, little is known about functional sequences. The generation of large sequence data sets will benefit from further advances in sequencing technology that significantly reduces costs.

Increasingly, powerful computational capacities will be required for robust computational infrastructure to hold and analyze data sets. High-throughput technologies should aim to complement the computational detection of functional elements.

Genes and gene products have complex, interconnected pathways that play a vital role in cellular behavior. This, in turn, impacts the workings of tissues, organs, and, finally, the organism itself. A proper understanding of this will require several levels of information. At gene and gene product levels, techniques that allow in vivo, real-time measurement of protein expression, localization, modification, and activity (kinetics) will be the key.

If all proteins in a cell can be monitored simultaneously, then protein pathways and systems biology can be better understood. A critical step will be to take an accurate census of the proteins present in particular cell types under different physiological conditions. This can be done in model systems such as microorganisms. A complete interaction map of the proteins in a cell and their cellular locations will be an atlas for the biological and medical explorations of cellular metabolism for centuries to come.

Policy options should be developed to facilitate the widespread use of genome information in both research and clinical settings. Researchers, commercial enterprises, healthcare providers, patients, and the public must have effective access to information on genomics, with researchers getting maximum and immediate access to the data. Intellectual property (IP) issues and commercialization will be complex. IP practices, laws, and regulations that affect genomics must adhere to the principle of maximizing public benefit, but must also be consistent with general IP principles.

Enhancing Data Storage

The biggest commercial systems available can handle about 300 terabytes (1,000 gigabytes or trillions of bits) of information. It is estimated that the size of computing power needed to fully analyze the human genome data will be measured in petabytes (1,000 terabytes). Here are some amazing numbers to come to terms with. One petabyte of information (one quadrillion bytes, or 1,000 terabytes) is the equivalent of 250 billion pages of text; 20 million four-drawer filing cabinets; 500 million high-density floppy disks; 83,000 digitally stored, feature-length movies; or 1.7 million CD-ROMs of information.

Those are massive storage requirements, so solution providers must create an integrated stake with technology companies and work together. Bioinformatics companies design tools and strategies to take the DNA sequencing data, either from the HGP or individual samples, and use computerized analysis to turn it into information that can be used in research. As of now, the human genome database has about three terabytes of data, enough to fill 150 million pages. With the amount of genetic data expected to double every six months in the foreseeable future, the demand for IT solutions should experience similar growth. The emerging IT infrastructure will include middleware that links different information from different databases, analytical applications that sort and organize the genetic data, and systems that will help store and distribute the collected information.

Harnessing the quantum properties of subatomic particles have led to some breathtaking possibilities in information processing and storage. As devices become smaller, the principles of quantum mechanics become increasingly more important. Consequently, aspects of genuine quantum information processing could soon begin to be commercially viable.

For instance, a group of researchers in the United States are doing pioneering work on the transfer of quantum information encoded in laser beams into a physical system, and the subsequent retrieval of that information unaltered. Another group is enthusiastic about trying to encode the entire contents of the Library of Congress in one electron by making use of its wave nature. This has brought the dream of quantum computing ever closer to reality.

The data storage capacities that can be achieved by quantum computing are virtually unlimited. However, such devices are not set to storm the market before the end of the decade at least. Quantum electronics is still in the realm of the exotic.

For a market that is already a decade old, bio-informatics still holds a lot of promise. The field offers

137

innumerable possibilities that could impact pharmaceuticals and healthcare in the near future. The increased market activity of some of the leading players is a testimony to this.

More than "if," it is a question of "what all?" and "when?"

Genes and Disease

5

About every 100 to 300 bases along the 3.1 billion-base-long human genome, a change occurs in the nucleotide sequence. These changes, called single nucleotide polymorphisms (SNPs), though infinitesimally small, are responsible for the majority of genetic variation in humans. Some SNPs can make a person more susceptible to diseases such as cancer or diabetes; others can cause a person to have an allergic reaction to a particular medicine.

Because SNPs can influence our health so profoundly and because they change little as genes are passed down from one generation to the next, scientists are studying them with great interest. They are using SNPs to better understand the causes of disease and to develop new and improved methods for treating those diseases.

This article by science writer Peter Gwynne highlights some of the current and future directions in SNP research. SNP maps are helping scientists learn how certain genes interact to *increase a person's susceptibility to disease. They are also aiding in the development of personalized medicines. In the future, drugs may be tailored precisely to an individual's DNA (a science called pharmacogenomics) to reduce the risk of harmful side effects and increase their effectiveness. —SW*

"Using SNP Analysis for a Clinical Look at Diseases"
by Peter Gwynne
Drug Discovery & Development, January 1, 2003

The sequencing of human and other genomes has opened the way to the rational use of genetic and genomic information in understanding the causes of diseases and developing treatments for them. Critical to that work, and to general understanding of genomics, are the detection and identification of the small genetic variations known as single-nucleotide polymorphisms (SNPs).

"There's a tremendous amount of excitement and interest in SNP analysis," says Greg Yap, senior director of marketing for DNA analysis at Affymetrix, Santa Clara, Calif. "This will be a new growth area for the field in general and for Affymetrix." Dennis Gilbert, vice president of genomics at Applied Biosystems Group, Foster City, Calif., agrees. "In terms of market potential we expect a great deal of compounded growth over the next few years," he says. "Investigating the human genome and finding commercially important targets will be like the Oklahoma land grab," says Charles Cantor, chief scientific officer of Sequenom Inc., San Diego. "Two years from now, everybody will be able to do this with various technologies."

Gilbert says that scientists should be cautious of the promise of SNPs. Clinical researchers pioneered the way to understanding the genetic bases of disease in the distant past. For example, a century ago physicians knew that certain symptoms such as a salty taste on the skin gave a differential diagnosis for cystic fibrosis. "Plainly something was wrong with salt transport," he says. "When they found the gene for cystic fibrosis, it turned out to be a salt transport gene. Clinical researchers look first for things that make sense, [such as] a pathway or a gene about which they have some suspicion."

SNPs have boosted that ability to find answers that make sense, but even they have some history behind them. "The SNP market is a new and growing market," says Gilbert. "But you shouldn't let the marketing and media people rename something that already existed. Pharmaceutical companies for many years looked at genes that were SNPs."

The difference between now and then, of course, is in the quantity of SNPs available to examine. The sequencing of the human genome has vastly increased the number of SNPs available to life scientists. In response, several methods of detecting SNPs have become available, as have applications of the knowledge gained by detecting them. Beyond exploring the genetic bases of diseases, says Gilbert, "there's a whole host of 'candidate' applications in understanding genes, pathways, and regions." Says Affymetrix's Yap, "Applications include gene resequencing, gene mapping, pharmacogenomics uses, and looking at bacteria. We're only at the beginning of defining the applications." Even agricultural researchers have shown interest in using SNP analysis.

SNPs are variations that occur when a single nucleotide in the genome sequence is changed. Thus, an SNP might alter the sequence AAGGCTAA to ATGGCTAA by the substitution of a thymine base for an adenine base (underlined position). SNPs are hardly rare events. They occur once in every 100 to 300 bases in the 3 billion bases that constitute the human genome, for example. They have less than a 1% effect on cellular function, because most SNPs appear outside the coding sequences of genomes. However, those SNPs that appear within the coding sequences hold out great interest for life scientists, as they promise to provide clues to the ways in which genetic changes affect cellular function and individuals' predispositions to disease and their response to drugs.

It is the effect of changes in DNA on the ways in which individuals respond to disease and environmental insults such as bacteria, viruses, toxins, and chemicals, as well as drugs, that makes SNPs so attractive to researchers. Amplifying that attraction is the fact that SNPs are relatively stable; they change little from generation to generation, which makes it easy for researchers to monitor them in population studies.

SNPs offer the research and biomedical communities particular value because most diseases stem from variations in more than one gene. Conventional genetic investigations permit scientists to identify disease conditions caused by single genes but run into difficulty when they encounter the majority of common ailments that are influenced by complex interactions among several genes, in addition to external factors. SNP maps promise to help researchers pick out the multiple genes involved in the patients' genetic predispositions to such diseases as cancer, diabetes, vascular ailments, and certain mental illnesses. Similarly, SNPs will help medical scientists identify individuals' differing reactions to various drugs, and to understand why those reactions occur.

Each person has a unique SNP pattern in her or his genome. Medical researchers can identify the SNPs common to individuals with particular diseases or specific adverse reactions to drugs. On occasion, SNPs themselves cause a disease. In those cases, the SNPs can be used to find and isolate the gene responsible for causing the disease. More often, though, SNPs are not themselves responsible for a particular disease state. Rather, they serve as markers that pinpoint a disease on the map of the human genome because they are frequently located on the genome near genes that are associated in some way with specific diseases.

Using SNPs to screen for a disease in cases in which the responsible gene has been identified is relatively simple. Scientists first look for SNPs in the DNA of patients affected by the disease, then they compare the readings with those from individuals not affected by the disease. These association studies reveal differences between the SNP patterns in the two groups, thus indicating the pattern of SNPs that is more likely to be associated with the gene responsible for the disease.

A major part of the effort to identify, catalog, and use SNPs is the assembly of SNP databases. Pharmaceutical and biotechnology firms develop their own private databases. But those firms' scientists, as well as academic researchers, are also using public SNP databases such as the dbSNP database set up by the National Center for Biotechnology Information (NCBI), of the National Institutes of Health (NIH), Bethesda, Md. The dbSNP links directly to several software tools designed to facilitate SNP analysis. For example, each SNP record in the database links to further resources in NCBI's "discovery space." They include GenBank, which is NIH's sequence database, LocusLink, a system that contains details of genes and associated information, NCBI's dbSTS, which contains sequence and mapping data on short genomic landmarks (sequence tagged sites), and PubMed, NCBI's system that searches for and retrieves literature. The overall result, according to NCBI, gives scientists the opportunity to do "one-stop SNP shopping."

Vendors are concentrating on making as many SNPs as possible available to the research and medical communities. "Customers ask what SNPs you have. That's how we've approached the market," says Gilbert of Applied Biosystems. "We've made SNPs that cover the entire genome and entire genes. If you make assays to every gene in the genome, that's good; every customer segment will pull down some of those assays."

Yet, Gilbert says, "We don't expect that one customer will want them all." The typical customer wants to see no more than about 200 genes in perhaps 200 patients. "Customers want to see all the SNPs in a disease pathway, or all the genes in one family," he says. Those customers come from a variety of backgrounds. They include academics carrying out research on diseases in moderately funded laboratories, discovery scientists in large pharmaceutical firms, and clinical researchers with well-characterized patients who might want to make some associations involving SNPs.

Quantity has its value in reducing the relative cost of SNP analysis. "The world of yesterday in SNP analysis was a candidate SNP world; you looked at SNPs you knew or strongly suspected were associated with diseases," says Yap of Affymetrix. "The method was somewhat complicated, had a high cost per SNP, and was not very flexible. The world of tomorrow in SNP analysis will involve high density analysis. More information, we believe, drives better results. Having a broader field of view gives customers much higher confidence in their results and that the conclusions they come to are correct. The fundamental shift we're starting to see is that people will take a broader field of view approach."

Affymetrix has responded to that shift by launching its CustomSeq product line, including an array that covers 10,000 SNPs. "CustomSeq is our first commercial product to do resequencing," says Yap. "It does 60 kb [kilobases] of sequence—30 kb on both strands—in a single hybridization and a single experiment. It will enable scientists to look at much more sequence information in a fast, more economical way." The new array is based on Affymetrix's high-density technology. "It has the highest number of SNPs available in a commercial product," says Yap. "Most people using SNPs use up to about 3,000. We're lifting the bar a bit." At present, the array is available for early access to select customers.

Imagine inserting a healthy gene into a person's body to replace a malfunctioning disease gene; removing cells from a damaged liver or kidney, engineering them in a laboratory, and then putting them back into the person's body to fix the damaged organ; or using a single cell or groups of cells from an embryo to grow new skin—even a whole ear—or fixing a heart defect with a tiny mechanical part.

These ideas may sound like science fiction, but they are becoming reality, thanks to regenerative medicine. Whereas medicines today are one size fits all and can usually do nothing more than slow or hide the progression of disease to make us feel better, regenerative medicine can actually change the body to fix damaged tissue or cure a disease permanently.

Author William A. Haseltine knows firsthand the promise of regenerative medicine. His company, Human Genome Sciences, studies human genes to develop new treatments and cures for diseases such as cancer, arthritis, and hepatitis C. In this article, he highlights the four types of regenerative medicine, revealing their current limitations—and their promise for the future of medicine. —SW

"Regenerative Medicine"
by William A. Haseltine
Brookings Review, January 1, 2003

The era of regenerative medicine is upon us. Rapidly advancing medical knowledge is leading to the development of powerful new gene-based therapies that will transform medical practice, allowing most people to live much longer and healthier lives.

Unlike most medicines today, regenerative medicines use human cells and substances to regrow tissue. Early forms are already in use. Some 30 drugs based on human proteins are approved for sale in the United States, as are several therapies that contain human cells. But today's protein and cell-based drugs are merely the harbingers of what is to come.

Over the past decade, the new science of genomics has made it possible to identify thousands of previously unknown human proteins. Thanks to high-speed, high-capacity laboratory robots, we can make those proteins in pure form, using standard biotechnology techniques. We can test their effects on human cells with relative ease and then evaluate the proteins that have potentially useful medical properties as possible cures. Today, many human-protein drugs identified through genomics are being evaluated in clinical trials.

There are four broad types of regenerative medicine: human substances (proteins and genes), cells and tissues, embryonic stem cells, and novel materials.

Human Substances

The first type of regenerative medicine involves the use of human proteins and genes as drugs. The proteins are generally made using recombinant DNA technology, sometimes known as gene splicing. Genes are chemical instructions that enable a cell to make a specific substance. If we transfer a functioning human gene into a cell that we can easily culture in large numbers, those cells will produce the desired human substance, often a hormone, in industrial quantities. Proteins made this way, unlike those extracted from human tissues, will not transmit infectious agents from a donor.

Current type 1 regenerative medicines include such important recombinant drugs as human insulin, interferon, human growth hormone, and erythropoietin, a substance that stimulates the formation of red blood cells. Because the body readily accepts another person's purified substances, protein drugs made from one person's gene can treat anyone. No major technical barriers remain to developing new human-protein drugs.

Some therapeutic proteins substitute for ones that patients cannot make themselves. Most patients with insulin dependent diabetes, for example, now use recombinant human insulin to compensate for their inability to make insulin, thereby regaining control over the amount of sugar in their blood. Other therapeutic proteins supplement the body's own inadequate production. Extra erythropoietin, for example, stimulates production of red blood cells in people undergoing chemotherapy for cancer and in people with kidney disease. Several types of supplemental recombinant interferon are now major pharmaceutical products. Interferon alpha is used to treat hepatitis and cancer; it stimulates the immune system to fight disease. Interferon beta treats multiple sclerosis, a disease in which a patient's immune system erroneously attacks his or her brain and spinal cord. It blunts the immune system's attack on the nervous system, easing patients' symptoms and probably lengthening lives.

Many more of the thousands of human proteins revealed by genomics are likely to have profound medical effects. The Human Genome Project, an international effort funded by governments and private organizations, recently produced a map and a draft text of the entirety of our human genetic information, known as the genome. Although much work remains before a definitive version is available, the effort will in time place all human substances within our grasp.

The Human Genome Project produces data about genes in their stored form in our chromosomes. Recognizing genes in this stored form is difficult, and many thousands of genes, known to exist through independent investigations, have thus far eluded the project. Researchers at my company, Human Genome Sciences, focus on isolating the active form of genes—so-called messenger RNA—that is produced only in a cell that is using the gene. They then convert the messenger RNA to a stable chemical copy, called a cDNA, which they examine to learn which genes are active in a variety of healthy and diseased tissues. The approach offers a rapid route to regenerative medicines. Our cDNAs have already yielded genes and proteins that function as active therapeutics.

Having identified, for example, chemical signals that the body uses to stimulate the formation of new skin, we now manufacture one of those signal substances as a healing protein drug called repifermin. Repifermin's demonstrated ability to heal leg ulcers is being further tested, and the drug is being evaluated as a treatment for chemotherapy-induced ulcers in the mouth and intestines.

Another Human Genome Sciences protein drug, called BLyS (pronounced "Bliss"), is an important, natural hormone that boosts blood levels of antibodies, specialized proteins that bind exceedingly tightly to a specific molecular target. We are testing BLyS as a treatment for diseases in which patients produce too few antibodies, making them more susceptible to disease.

Indeed, antibodies, an essential arm of the immune system, are themselves used as a form of type 1 regenerative medicine. Their ability to bind to a target tightly allows them to inactivate harmful substances in the body and makes them valuable for treating autoimmune illnesses like rheumatoid arthritis and Crohn's disease, which are triggered by an overreaction of the immune system. Medicine can also create antibodies that bind to and activate specific receptors on cells. That binding property makes it possible to activate a receptor without using the natural protein that would normally bind to it. This is a sound strategy when the natural protein is unsuitable for use as a drug. For example, Human Genome Sciences has been approved to test in patients an antibody that binds to the so-called Trail 1 "death receptor" found on cancer cells. When a natural protein called Trail binds to the receptor, the cancer cells die. Trail itself cannot be used as a drug, but our antibody mimics its effects; it may become an important medicine for several types of cancer.

For some conditions, regenerative medicine will use genes themselves as medicines. Genes last indefinitely in cells, meaning that once a therapeutic extra gene is in place in a cell, the effects should last as long as the cell does—months or even years—thus eliminating the need for frequent medication. Several perplexing problems, however, still bedevil gene therapy, making its future somewhat uncertain. For example, it is a challenge to protect genes, once they are inserted, from the body's defenses, and to direct them to the place in the body where they would do the most good. Although gene therapies have produced good results in clinical tests with a small number of patients, it could be many years before they are widely used.

Conventional, chemically-based drugs serve mostly as temporary supports for the body's failing chemistry. They usually do not repair what is wrong. If a patient with a tendency to depression stops taking medication, for example, the depression returns. Nor do chemically based drugs regenerate injured or worn tissues. Regenerative medicine, by contrast, has the potential to cure disease, because it can bring about long-lasting changes in the body that are tailored to a particular ailment. Regenerative medicines generally also have less toxic effects than chemical drugs, because they are based on natural substances. They are also less likely to cause dangerous side effects when used in combination with other drugs.

The many drugs based on human substances such as hormones, antibodies, and genes that are now being tested are only the beginning of what will become a far-reaching revolution.

Cells and Tissues

As we become comfortable using human substances as medicines, we are also starting to use human cells as medicine. In type 2 regenerative medicine, cells will be removed from the body, grown in culture, then reintroduced into patients.

Type 2 regenerative medicine is often referred to as a form of tissue engineering. The field evolved from reconstructive surgery, the rebuilding of damaged body parts. Tissue engineering takes two forms. One involves building an organ or tissue outside the body by combining human cells with appropriate materials, often a scaffold-like structure to provide support. The other involves growing suitable cells in laboratory flasks, then injecting them into a tissue needing repair. The cells can often find their own way to the sites where they are needed. Some of the human substances discovered in type 1 help in type 2, because they can direct cells to change, migrate, and divide.

Progress in tissue engineering is accelerating dramatically. The need for replacement organs and tissues is growing, driven in part by the aging of the population. Among older people, diseased or worn-out muscle, bone, cartilage, nerves, digestive systems, skin, and brain cells may all benefit from cell based interventions. We can already culture many human cells, including elusive but powerful adult stem cells, outside the body. Adult stem cells have prized potential for healing because they can renew themselves indefinitely.

The secret of growing many replacement tissues seems to lie in providing intricate scaffolds, foundations on which cells may grow. Several natural and synthetic substances are proving valuable for creating structures that mimic natural scaffolds, and we are rapidly learning how to use such structures to create working tissues.

Companies now use human cells to make artificial skin, a product that has considerably improved care of burn victims. Another firm prepares a cell-based therapy for joint repair from patients' own cultured cells. Scientists can also grow new blood vessels in the laboratory, as well as cardiac muscle, corneas, and parts of the alimentary canal, the urogenital system, liver, and kidney. Clinicians are starting to implant these new tissues into patients.

Bone marrow transplants have for decades been used to regenerate marrow tissue destroyed by chemotherapy and radiotherapy. Surgeons rescue patients by transplanting replacement bone marrow stem cells, which migrate to suitable sites in the bones and permanently spawn new blood cells. This therapy gives hope that we will be able to develop many more adult stem cell therapies.

Indeed, bone marrow stem cells appear to have greater potential than anyone suspected, for they can apparently turn into other types of stem cells. Stem cells of various kinds are under investigation for repairing injuries to the spinal cord, bone, brain, and other organs. Brain stem cells are showing particular promise. Isolating enough stem cells is often a challenge, so bone marrow stem cells may play an important role as progenitors of multiple stem cell types.

Patients who receive medicines derived from cells that are not their own must sometimes be given immunosuppressive drugs to prevent rejection of the foreign cells. Yet not all types of tissue prompt immune rejection, so for some tissue transplants immunosuppressive drugs are unnecessary. Furthermore, banks of tissues with diverse immune characteristics will likely be established, making it possible to select a close match for any given patient's tissue. Type 2 regenerative medicine therapies may well find widespread application within the next decade. Brain stem cells may find broad uses even sooner.

Eventually, many more types of stem cells will be in medical use. And developments in materials science suggest we will be able to use cells in more varied ways before long. Evolving fabrication techniques could soon make it possible to engineer scaffolds to a precision of a few atomic diameters. Materials made with such precision—comparable to that of the body itself—will offer much greater control over the growth of cells, and so will expand the range of conditions that cell-based medicine can treat.

Despite its promise, type 2 regenerative medicine remains limited by the difficulty of isolating and activating adult stem cells. To repair some tissues for which bone marrow or other adult stem cells are inapplicable or unavailable, we may have to turn to a more powerful type of cell, the embryonic stem cell.

Embryonic Stem Cells

The third type of regenerative medicine, which will be distinct both from the use of human substances as drugs and from tissue engineering as described so far, does not yet exist. Yet the key discoveries that will enable it to develop have already been made, so it will arrive in due course—if society permits.

The defining feature of type 3 regenerative medicine is embryonic stem cells, special cells obtained from very early-stage human embryos. These cells can develop into every major kind of cell in the body (more than 200 cell types exist in the body). They have already been coaxed into establishing cultures of many different kinds of potentially healing cells, including several types of nerve cells, heart muscle, skin cells, and certain immune-system cells. That virtuoso flexibility stands in contrast to the much more limited potential of most adult stem cells, which will probably be limited to only certain cell types.

Cultures of embryonic stem cells can be maintained for years, thus in principle overcoming the main obstacle slowing development of type 2 regenerative medicine—isolating and growing enough adult stem cells. Embryonic stem cells have extraordinary potential for repairing and regenerating damaged or worn-out organs.

Although mouse embryonic stem cells have long been known, the human version was found only in 1998. Which type of tissue these cells give rise to depends on which specific human substances they are exposed to as they grow. Researchers, however, have not yet established precisely how to make them turn efficiently and predictably into many of the specific cell types needed. This must be the key research goal for the future.

Embryonic stem cells have been used successfully to treat injury and illness in animals, including spinal cord injuries in rats. They have also shown promise treating rodents with conditions that mimic Alzheimer's disease and Parkinson's disease. Potential benefits are not restricted to the brain and nerve cells. Cells made from embryonic stem cells can survive in the pancreas and secrete insulin and even withstand attack by the mouse immune system well enough to reverse diabetes. Naturally, the hope is that the equivalent human cells will do the same for human patients.

Embryonic stem cells, like many adult stem cells, trigger an immune reaction when injected into an organism that is not a genetic match. Their use thus might depend, as a practical matter, on a powerful new biological technique known as nuclear transplantation, which was used in 1997 to produce Dolly, the cloned sheep.

Nuclear transplantation should in principle be able to produce early-stage embryos that are genetically identical to any patient's cell sample, thus eliminating the difficulty of obtaining genetically compatible cells. In cloning animals, the nucleus from one cell of the creature is removed and transferred to an egg of the same species from which the nucleus has been removed. An electric shock causes the egg to start developing into an early embryo. Implanted in a womb, the embryo will sometimes develop into a cloned offspring genetically identical to the animal that supplied the original nucleus. But if the objective is to derive stem cells, the cells are extracted from the very early-stage embryo, which is not implanted into a womb.

The Dolly experiment proved two important points. One was that we can "reprogram" an adult cell so that its descendants can turn into any other type of cell in the body. Dolly also showed that nuclear transplantation can rejuvenate aging cells, setting back their internal "clock" so that they act like young cells once again—a process that might be used to rejuvenate aging human cells.

The idea of exploiting rejuvenation in medicine is not as remote as it might at first appear. Bone marrow transplant recipients are routinely given cells from a much younger person, and the cells thrive. Type 3 regenerative medicine that uses nuclear transplantation to produce matched embryonic stem cells could become an important part of the medical scene.

However, it is uncertain whether society will fully assist research into embryonic stem cells and nuclear transplantation any time soon. The Bush administration has restricted federal support for research on embryonic stem cells to a small set of established cell lines, which may or may not be medically useful. Because nuclear transplantation could be used to make a copy of a human being, some people oppose any use of that technique, including the therapeutic, not reproductive, uses that the vast majority of scientists envision for it. The Bush administration has supported attempts to ban any use of nuclear transplantation to create tissues that match those of a patient. Unless these positions are reversed, the United States will fall behind the rest of the world in these exceptionally promising areas.

Opposition to using embryonic stem cells derives from their origin in embryos, which are destroyed as cells are retrieved. Yet at this early stage of development the microscopic human embryo, consisting of perhaps fewer than 100 cells, has no heart, no brain, and no nervous system to feel pain. In vitro fertilization programs produce—and dispose of—thousands of such embryos every year in excess of those that women can carry to term. Often donors would be willing to volunteer an embryo otherwise destined for disposal to supply stem cells for healing the sick.

Nuclear transplantation is likewise a technique that people ought to be able to choose. Current attempts to prevent nuclear transplantation to produce human embryonic stem cells are retarding the development of medicines that could greatly enhance the quality of life, or save the lives, of potentially millions of people.

Novel Materials

Rapid progress in materials science underlies type 4 regenerative medicine, in which novel materials engineered to atomic-scale precision will integrate seamlessly with our own cells. Functioning microscopic devices and other structures produced by atomic-scale engineering will be able to meld with the body without causing rejection. In becoming part of us, these creations will provide the aged and the sick with restored capabilities unthinkable with cells and human substances alone. Indeed, we can expect that they will surpass the body's natural capabilities. The implications of atomic-scale engineering, or nanotechnology, are far-reaching. Medical applications will boost regenerative medicine far beyond anything we can achieve today.

The field will take time to mature, but its earliest beginnings can already be discerned. Physicians commonly implant steel or plastic hip joints, synthetic heart valves, and dacron blood vessels. Thousands of people hear with artificial cochleas within their inner ears.

What sort of substance can be made to fuse with the body? The answer is surprisingly simple: any material that persists in the body and does not attract the attention of the immune system. That defensive system, composed of specialized blood cells as well as antibodies, will reject materials that it recognizes as chemically different from the body's natural components. Yet it will accept those that are chemically similar and will even accept some materials that do not resemble our components, provided they carry no chemical red flags to attract attention.

Devices and prostheses that can fuse with the body must be made of carefully selected materials. Experiments have identified several that are suitable, including certain minerals and the alloyed metals used in shoulder and hip replacements, as well as some plastic-like substances that eventually dissolve in the body, such as those used during surgery as temporary fastenings.

Recent achievements in micromechanical engineering, electronics, and materials science hold much promise for the future of implanted devices. For example, at the heart of spy satellites are coin-sized devices that contain more than a million individual detectors. In medical applications, they could be used, and are being tested, as artificial retinas.

Although society has been slow to put its best efforts into helping the disabled, new avenues appear promising. Researchers have amplified signals in the brains of patients and translated them into movements of a mechanical arm. This progress suggests that signals from a paralyzed patient's brain could, with appropriate feedback, achieve fine control over muscles, thereby bypassing injuries of the spinal cord.

It has been speculated that more refined implants could, in time, enhance our mental capacities. Prostheses that integrate with the nervous system might even bolster our memory and our analytical abilities. By connecting to external computers, such prostheses could fundamentally change our relationship to the material world. The ethical and philosophical implications of such changes are profound, although society has yet to pay much attention to such possibilities.

Given the advanced nature of such revolutionary technologies, it may be many years before prostheses engineered to atomic accuracy can take a crucial role in treating damage to the nervous system and other body systems. In the meantime, however, advances in atomic-scale engineering will accelerate type 2 and type 3 regenerative medicine.

From Regeneration to Rejuvenation

Chemical drugs have no effect on aging. Remarkably, however, regenerative medicines may very well be able to check the changes of aging. After all, they are the very substances and cells that steer our development and maintain and repair our bodies. They can stimulate the regrowth of aging tissues.

Regenerative medicine can already restore complex tissues. Repifermin, as noted, forms new skin. Recombinant human growth hormone promotes muscle growth. Drugs to regenerate skin and muscles could make an enormous difference to many of us as we age.

No single drug will treat all aspects of aging. But we can envisage a range of regenerative medicines for different symptoms. Human substances are now in testing for boosting the immune system, strengthening bones, repairing cartilage, and a variety of other purposes. As regenerative medicine advances, we will learn how to restore an ever-widening range of worn-out organs and tissues.

The choices society makes could speed—or slow—the arrival of these revolutionary therapies. Attempts to limit health care costs, in particular to contain the cost of pharmaceuticals, could strangle the emerging biotechnology industry, with disastrous effects for regenerative medicine.

Society faces difficult decisions about how to pay to translate advances in scientific knowledge into regenerative medicine. My own view is that we must move forward with maximum vigor to develop therapies that minimize human suffering. In the end, people will want to, and should be allowed to, make the choices that will give them happier, more productive, and longer lives.

Regenerative medicine may become the most powerful tool available to improve the human condition. Science has shown it can achieve the goal of using the body's own substances and cells to repair, restore, and rejuvenate it. Once society is fully aware of the staggering potential of regenerative medicine, it is unlikely to decline the promise that it offers.

Reprinted with permission from *Brookings Review*.

Several articles in this anthology have already focused on the promise of studying genes to identify disease risk. The new science of nutritional genomics offers a slight variation on that theme, by using genes as a tool to determine how diet can affect health.

Doctors have long known that the foods people eat can have a direct impact on their health. Nutritional genomics focuses on how genes and diet interact to cause or prevent disease. Just as the field of pharmacogenomics offers the possibility of personalized medicine, nutritional genomics offers the possibility of personalized diets. By analyzing a person's genetic makeup, doctors can match a diet exactly to the individual's health needs, modifying the intake of certain foods to prevent disease.

This article from The Economist *shows how nutritional genomics may someday change the way we eat. —SW*

"We Are What We Eat"
The Economist, September 6, 2003

Some people eat three-egg omelettes topped with slivers of bacon and show no sign of a spike in cholesterol. Others indulge in one chocolate bar after another and stay as thin as a rake. Many, however, are less fortunate. Current research suggests that the culprit may be found in one's genes. Differences in genetic make-up may not only determine the body's ability to metabolise certain nutrients, such as fats and lactose, but also its susceptibility to disease.

The good news is that, within five years or so, researchers should learn how to modify people's diets to fit their genes and thereby prevent or delay the onset of a possible illness. At least, that is the goal of nutritional genomics—a new field that studies how genes and diet interact.

Projects in nutritional genomics are sprouting around the globe. Europe is merging its efforts in the field by launching NuGO early next year, a network that aims to integrate and develop the new branch of research. In America, the National Institutes of Health recently granted the University of California at Davis $6.5m to establish a Centre of Excellence for Nutritional Genomics.

In addition, there are international projects under way, such as HapMap, that focus on studying the pattern of inheritance of single nucleotide polymorphisms or SNPs (pronounced "snips"). These are places where the message encoded in the genome may vary by a single genetic "letter" between individuals. SNPs may determine differences in appearance, such as hair and eye colour, predisposition to illnesses, and how people respond to foods and drugs. Nutrition will be an important part of the new paradigm of "personalised medicine" and preventive health care, says Craig Venter, who spearheaded a private effort to sequence the human genome, and is now collaborating with Duke University Medical Centre to include genomic information in health-care planning.

Only a few diseases are based on mutations in single genes—as is the case with, say, cystic fibrosis or Huntington's chorea. As scientists have learned more about the human genome, they have found that many illnesses, including cancer and type II diabetes, are the result of an interaction between a number of genes and their environment. More than 100 genes have been implicated in the development of coronary artery disease (though carrying only one such gene is still a risk factor). But to express those genes, there needs to be a trigger—such as diet. Researchers estimate that diet may be the defining factor in a third of all cancers.

A gene is a recipe for making a protein. At the molecular level, various nutrients interact with genes by binding to DNA transcription factors—which regulate gene expression. Thus, the amount and type of food consumed affects the production of proteins directly.

Similar to "pharmacogenomics," which studies the effects of common genetic variants on drug response, nutritional genomics investigates the effect of diets on different individuals, groups and populations. But unlike drugs—which come as refined compounds, are administered in specific doses and have relatively short-acting effects—foods, like genes, act in concert. "They're like a great big symphony," explains Wasyl Malyj, who directs the laboratory for high performance computing and informatics at Davis's new centre. Moreover, the effects of foods are slow moving—and often take years before becoming visible.

As a result, no one meal is ever going to be detrimental for most people. The trick will be to find out what constitutes the best balance of nutrients over long periods. For example, a recent paper in the *New England Journal of Medicine* describes the effects of a traditional Mediterranean diet—lots of olive oil, fresh fruits, vegetables, legumes and nuts, moderate amounts of fish and wine, and little meat and dairy products. Those who adhered closely to the diet lived longer and were less likely to die of heart disease or cancer. There was, however, no association between longevity and any individual food component of the diet.

The complexity of human nutrition poses challenges. Clinical trials require a large group of people to be followed over many years. That makes studies costly and hard to conduct. Moreover, people often forget what they have eaten.

But progress is being made thanks to "systems biology," which uses the tools of genomics, molecular biology and bioinformatics to study the complex inter-actions of genes, proteins and nutrients at the cellular level. DNA chips can now look at thousands of genes at once, allowing complex gene-expression profiles to be created quickly. In addition, studies of human cell cultures and "knockout mice," which lack the ability to make specific proteins, provide other means of col-lecting data. The goal is to find early molecular profiles ("biomarkers"), which may be a useful step on the way to identifying diseases before they pose health problems.

Changes in DNA have occurred in human popula-tions as evolutionary responses to changes in diet. For example, a change in a single gene 10,000 years ago allowed a group of northern Europeans to become lactose-tolerant and continue to consume milk products into adulthood. But such evolutionary responses take time. They also depend on the weeding out of inappropriate genes by the early deaths of carriers. In other words, they only happen because some genes cause diseases when exposed to the new diet.

For example, roughly half the adult population of the Pima tribe in Arizona have developed diabetes. This seems to be in response to a modern American diet, and its associated way of life. Another group of Pima, which lives in Mexico and still follows a more traditional diet and a less sedentary lifestyle, shows no significant increase in the disease. Singapore, with residents of Chinese, Indian and Malay descent who share similar prosperity and eating habits, serves as another interesting example. A portion of this ethnically-mixed population is now affected by the formerly uncommon coronary heart disease, but in unequal proportions—a result of a difference in genetic predisposition.

What is acceptable for one individual may actually harm another, says Ronald Krauss, director of atherosclerosis research at Children's Hospital Oakland, in California. Dr Krauss, who also chaired the American Heart Association's dietary guidelines committee in 2000, says its current recommendations benefit most people. However, it may be useful for some to adjust their diet based upon their genetic profile.

Dr Krauss, who has been researching the effects of various types of low-density lipoprotein (LDL), or "bad cholesterol," suggests that some healthy people may actually increase their risk of heart disease by embarking on an extremely low fat/high carbohydrate diet—something that is sometimes recommended as a way of lowering cholesterol. He has found that people with large LDL particles in their blood, a state of affairs that is relatively safe, can develop an abundance of small LDL particles, which is more dangerous, after a few weeks on such a diet.

One of the first projects of Davis's new centre will be to compare tissue samples from white and black American men. For reasons not yet understood, black American men have a 60 % higher incidence of prostate cancer than their white compatriots. Analysing the degree of genetic variations between the two groups may provide clues to the importance of environmental factors—such as diet and access to good health care—which could play a part in the disparity. Eventually, hopes Raymond Rodriguez, the director of the Davis centre, nutritional genomics will usher in a new era of consumer genetics that will translate into practical lifestyle changes and dietary choices.

Food as Medicine

Businesses certainly hope so. The current epidemic of metabolic diseases, such as obesity, diabetes and heart disease—in which diet is an important risk factor as well as a preventive agent—provides an opportunity for companies to develop foods that help populations at risk. Add to that the clinical proof of diet/gene interactions, and the traditional distinction between medicine and food becomes increasingly blurred. As a result, food companies may begin to think more like drug firms.

While they have only a fraction of the R&D budgets that pharmaceutical companies make available, some food companies are already marketing "functional foods" that address the needs of specific populations and have gone through independent clinical trials. One example is Unilever's Flora pro.activ—a bread spread that reduces cholesterol by 10–15%. Unilever, an Anglo-Dutch giant supplying foods and other consumer products globally, has formed a partnership with Perlegen, a genetics company based in Mountain View, California, which has catalogued no fewer than 1.5m common genetic variations in humans to date. The aim is to develop new foods that match the needs of specific populations. Nestle, the largest food company in the world, has similar agreements in place.

As more interactions between diet and genes become known, simple genetic tests via "cheek sweeps" (DNA testing based on swabbing the inside of the cheek) may determine what people need to eat. A handful of companies, such as Sciona in Britain, has already begun to sell products (available online and through some health-care providers) that test for genes that influence the metabolism of alcohol, folate and other nutrients. Based on the results, Sciona makes suggestions for diet modifications. But experts agree that, thus far, such tests have little meaning. "Telling somebody what to eat based on a few genes is not appropriate," says Jim Kaput, founder of NutraGenomics, a start-up that plans to offer genetic tests once the knowledge is more advanced.

However, before such tests become commonplace, a number of ethical, medical and legal issues will need to be addressed. One fear is that insurance companies might gain access to the information and charge higher premiums, or even exclude people from their plans, on the basis of their genes. And, because of the complexity of diet/gene interactions, it will be essential to train physicians to interpret the test results. Despite these hurdles, most researchers agree, the potential benefits outweigh the possible harm. As Dr. Ordovas, professor of nutrition and genetics at Tufts University in Massachusetts, says, predicting illnesses 40 or 50 years before they may arise is not only a convenient way to minimise the need for expensive drugs—but also a powerful tool to improve the quality of a person's life.

Modifying Nature with Genetics

6

Our knowledge of animal and plant genes has progressed to the point where we can actually manipulate the genetic material of an organism to change it or alter the way it functions. This science, called genetic engineering, is as promising as it is controversial. Proponents say genetic engineering will create bigger, hardier, safer, and more nutritious foods to nourish an ever-growing world population. Detractors argue that genetic engineering is akin to playing God and that it could have dangerous consequences for the health and safety of millions of people.

In the following article, science writer Jennifer Ackerman discusses some of the ways in which scientists are using genetic engineering today and introduces some potential applications for this relatively new science in the future. The many scientists and researchers interviewed for the story illustrate the debate by highlighting the many possible benefits and potential risks of genetic engineering. —SW

"Food: How Altered?"
by Jennifer Ackerman
National Geographic, **May 1, 2002**

As this global industry expands and evolves, scientists and consumers are raising more and more questions. How can we keep our food supply safe? And what might be the benefits and risks of ever accelerating advances in genetic engineering?

The simple act of planting by hand, though still practiced by millions in India and other developing nations, seems increasingly archaic in the face of big-business agriculture.

Cooked Right?

Behind each order for a sausage-and-pepper sandwich at the New York State Fair in Syracuse lies a customer's trust that the food will not make him sick. State and county inspectors monitor meat temperatures and sanitary conditions. Yet guaranteeing the safety of meats and produce has become an increasingly complex and uncertain proposition as Americans more than ever depend on food produced and prepared outside the home.

What Happens When It's Changed

Two month old coho salmon show the difference genetic engineering can make. The top fish [illustrated in the original article] has been given a modified gene that lets it grow at a faster pace, while its counterpart grows more slowly in winter. As producers move to bring fast-growing salmon to market, biologist Bob Devlin assesses the risks the fish would pose to natural populations if they escaped into the wild. "I've been working with these animals for ten years, and I don't know."

Scientists continue to find new ways to insert genes for specific traits into plant and animal DNA. A field of promise—and a subject of debate—genetic engineering is changing the food we eat and the world we live in.

In the brave new world of genetic engineering, Dean DellaPenna envisions this cornucopia: tomatoes and broccoli bursting with cancer-fighting chemicals and vitamin-enhanced crops of rice, sweet potatoes, and cassava to help nourish the poor. He sees wheat, soy, and peanuts free of allergens; bananas that deliver vaccines; and vegetable oils so loaded with therapeutic ingredients that doctors "prescribe" them for patients at risk for cancer and heart disease. A plant biochemist at Michigan State University, DellaPenna believes that genetically engineered foods are the key to the next wave of advances in agriculture and health.

While DellaPenna and many others see great potential in the products of this new biotechnology, some see uncertainty, even danger. Critics fear that genetically engineered products are being rushed to market before their effects are fully understood. Anxiety has been fueled by reports of taco shells contaminated with genetically engineered corn not approved for human consumption; the potential spread of noxious "superweeds" spawned by genes picked up from engineered crops; and possible harmful effects of biotech corn pollen on monarch butterflies.

In North America and Europe the value and impact of genetically engineered food crops have become subjects of intense debate, provoking reactions from unbridled optimism to fervent political opposition.

Just what are genetically engineered foods, and who is eating them? What do we know about their benefits—and their risks? What effect might engineered plants have on the environment and on agricultural practices around the world? Can they help feed and preserve the health of the Earth's burgeoning population?

Q: Who's eating biotech foods?

A: In all likelihood, you are.

Most people in the United States don't realize that they've been eating genetically engineered foods since the mid-1990s. More than 60 percent of all processed foods on U.S. supermarket shelves—including pizza, chips, cookies, ice cream, salad dressing, corn syrup, and baking powder—contain ingredients from engineered soybeans, corn, or canola.

In the past decade or so, the biotech plants that go into these processed foods have leaped from hothouse oddities to crops planted on a massive scale—on 130 million acres in 13 countries, among them Argentina, Canada, China, South Africa, Australia, Germany, and Spain. On U.S. farmland, acreage planted with genetically engineered crops jumped nearly 25-fold from 3.6 million acres in 1996 to 88.2 million acres in 2001. More than 50 different "designer" crops have passed through a federal review process, and about a hundred more are undergoing field trials.

Q: How long have we been genetically altering our food?

A: Longer than you think.

Genetic modification is not novel. Humans have been altering the genetic makeup of plants for millennia, keeping seeds from the best crops and planting them in following years, breeding and crossbreeding varieties to make them taste sweeter, grow bigger, last longer. In this way we've transformed the wild tomato, Lycopersicon, from a fruit the size of a marble to today's giant, juicy beefsteaks. From a weedy plant called teosinte with an "ear" barely an inch long has come our foot-long ears of sweet white and yellow corn. In just the past few decades plant breeders have used traditional techniques to produce varieties of wheat and rice plants with higher grain yields. They have also created hundreds of new crop variants using irradiation and mutagenic chemicals.

But the technique of genetic engineering is new, and quite different from conventional breeding. Traditional breeders cross related organisms whose genetic makeups are similar. In so doing, they transfer tens of thousands of genes. By contrast, today's genetic engineers can transfer just a few genes at a time between species that are distantly related or not related at all.

Genetic engineers can pull a desired gene from virtually any living organism and insert it into virtually any other organism. They can put a rat gene into lettuce to make a plant that produces vitamin C or splice genes from the cecropia moth into apple plants, offering protection from fire blight, a bacterial disease that damages apples and pears. The purpose is the same: to insert a gene or genes from a donor organism carrying a desired trait into an organism that does not have the trait.

The engineered organisms scientists produce by transferring genes between species are called transgenic. Several dozen transgenic food crops are currently on the market, among them varieties of corn, squash, canola, soybeans, and cotton, from which cottonseed oil is produced. Most of these crops are engineered to help farmers deal with age-old agriculture problems: weeds, insects, and disease.

Farmers spray herbicides to kill weeds. Biotech crops can carry special "tolerance" genes that help them withstand the spraying of chemicals that kill nearly every other kind of plant. Some biotech varieties make their own insecticide, thanks to a gene borrowed from a common soil bacterium, Bacillus thuringiensis, or Bt for short.

Bt genes code for toxins considered to be harmless to humans but lethal to certain insects, including the European corn borer, an insect that tunnels into cornstalks and ears, making it a bane of corn farmers. So effective is Bt that organic farmers have used it as a natural insecticide for decades, albeit sparingly. Corn borer caterpillars bite into the leaves, stems, or kernels of a Bt corn plant, the toxin attacks their digestive tracts, and they die within a few days.

Other food plants—squash and papaya, for instance—have been genetically engineered to resist diseases. Lately scientists have been experimenting with potatoes, modifying them with genes of bees and moths to protect the crops from potato blight fungus, and grapevines with silkworm genes to make the vines resistant to Pierce's disease, spread by insects.

With the new tools of genetic engineering, scientists have also created transgenic animals. Atlantic salmon grow more slowly during the winter, but engineered salmon, "souped-up" with modified growth-hormone genes from other fish, reach market size in about half the normal time. Scientists are also using biotechnology to insert genes into cows and sheep so that the animals will produce pharmaceuticals in their milk. None of these transgenic animals have yet entered the market.

Q: Are biotech foods safe for humans?

A: Yes, as far as we know.

"Risks exist everywhere in our food supply," points out Dean DellaPenna. "About a hundred people die each year from peanut allergies. With genetically engineered foods we minimize risks by doing rigorous testing."

According to Eric Sachs, a spokesman for Monsanto, a leading developer of biotech products: "Transgenic products go through more testing than any of the other foods we eat. We screen for potential toxins and allergens. We monitor the levels of nutrients, proteins, and other components to see that the transgenic plants are substantially equivalent to traditional plants."

Three federal agencies regulate genetically engineered crops and foods—the U.S. Department of Agriculture (USDA), the Environmental Protection Agency (EPA), and the Food and Drug Administration (FDA). The FDA reviews data on allergens, toxicity, and nutrient levels voluntarily submitted by companies. If that information shows that the new foods are not substantially equivalent to conventional ones, the foods must undergo further testing. Last year the agency proposed tightening its scrutiny of engineered foods, making the safety assessments mandatory rather than voluntary.

"When it comes to addressing concerns about health issues, industry is being held to very high standards," says DellaPenna, "and it's doing its best to meet them in reasonable and rigorous fashion."

In the mid-1990s a biotech company launched a project to insert a gene from the Brazil nut into a soybean. The Brazil nut gene selected makes a protein rich in one essential amino acid. The aim was to create a more nutritious soybean for use in animal feed. Because the Brazil nut is known to contain an allergen, the company also tested the product for human reaction, with the thought that the transgenic soybean might accidentally enter the human food supply. When tests showed that humans would react to the modified soybeans, the project was abandoned.

For some people this was good evidence that the system of testing genetically engineered foods works. But for some scientists and consumer groups, it raised the specter of allergens or other hazards that might slip through the safety net. Scientists know that some proteins, such as the one in the Brazil nut, can cause allergic reactions in humans, and they know how to test for these allergenic proteins. But the possibility exists that a novel protein with allergenic properties might turn up in an engineered food—just as it might in a new food produced by conventional means—and go undetected. Furthermore, critics say, the technique of moving genes across dramatically different species increases the likelihood of something going awry—either in the function of the inserted gene or in the function of the host DNA—raising the possibility of unanticipated health effects.

An allergy scare in 2000 centered around StarLink, a variety of genetically engineered corn approved by the U.S. government only for animal use because it showed some suspicious qualities, among them a tendency to break down slowly during digestion, a known characteristic of allergens. When StarLink found its way into taco shells, corn chips, and other foods, massive and costly recalls were launched to try to remove the corn from the food supply.

No cases of allergic response have been pinned to StarLink. In fact, according to Steve L. Taylor, chair of the Department of Food Science and Technology at the University of Nebraska, "None of the current biotech products have been implicated in allergic reactions or any other healthcare problem in people." Nevertheless, all new foods may present new risks. Only rigorous testing can minimize those risks.

Often overlooked in the debate about the health effects of these foods is one possible health benefit: Under some conditions corn genetically engineered for insect resistance may enhance safety for human and animal consumption. Corn damaged by insects often contains high levels of fumonisins, toxins made by fungi that are carried on the backs of insects and that grow in the wounds of the damaged corn. Lab tests have linked fumonisins with cancer in animals, and they may be potentially cancer-causing to humans. Among people who consume a lot of corn—in certain parts of South Africa, China, and Italy, for instance—there are high rates of esophageal cancer, which scientists associate with fumonisins. Studies show that most Bt corn has lower levels of fumonisins than conventional corn damaged by insects.

Should genetically engineered foods be labeled? Surveys suggest that most Americans would say yes (although they wouldn't want to pay more for the labeling). Professor Marion Nestle, chair of the Department of Nutrition and Food Studies at New York University, favors labeling because she believes consumers want to know and have the right to choose. However, no engineered foods currently carry labels in the U.S. because the FDA has not found any of them to be substantially different from their conventional counterparts. Industry representatives argue that labeling engineered foods that are not substantially different would arouse unwarranted suspicion.

Q: Can biotech foods harm the environment?

A: It depends on whom you ask.

Most scientists agree: The main safety issues of genetically engineered crops involve not people but the environment. "We've let the cat out of the bag before we have real data, and there's no calling it back," says Allison Snow, a plant ecologist at Ohio State University.

Snow is known for her research on "gene flow," the movement of genes via pollen and seeds from one population of plants to another, and she and some other environmental scientists worry that genetically engineered crops are being developed too quickly and released on millions of acres of farmland before they've been adequately tested for their possible long term ecological impact.

Advocates of genetically engineered crops argue that the plants offer an environmentally friendly alternative to pesticides, which tend to pollute surface and groundwater and harm wildlife. The use of Bt varieties has dramatically reduced the amount of pesticide applied to cotton crops. But the effects of genetic engineering on pesticide use with more widely grown crops are less clear-cut.

What might be the effect of these engineered plants on so-called nontarget organisms, the creatures that visit them? Concerns that crops with built-in insecticides might damage wildlife were inflamed in 1999 by the report of a study suggesting that Bt corn pollen harmed monarch butterfly caterpillars.

Monarch caterpillars don't feed on corn pollen, but they do feed on the leaves of milkweed plants, which often grow in and around cornfields. Entomologists at Cornell University showed that in the laboratory Bt corn pollen dusted onto milkweed leaves stunted or killed some of the monarch caterpillars that ate the leaves. For some environmental activists this was confirmation that genetically engineered crops were dangerous to wildlife. But follow-up studies in the field, reported last fall, indicate that pollen densities from Bt corn rarely reach damaging levels on milkweed, even when monarchs are feeding on plants within a cornfield.

"The chances of a caterpillar finding Bt pollen doses as high as those in the Cornell study are negligible," says Rick Hellmich, an entomologist with the Agricultural Research Service and one author of the follow-up report. "Butterflies are safer in a Bt cornfield than they are in a conventional cornfield, when they're subjected to chemical pesticides that kill not just caterpillars but most insects in the field."

Perhaps a bigger concern has to do with insect evolution. Crops that continuously make Bt may hasten the evolution of insects impervious to the pesticide. Such a breed of insect, by becoming resistant to Bt, would rob many farmers of one of their safest, most environmentally friendly tools for fighting the pests.

To delay the evolution of resistant insects, U.S. government regulators, working with biotech companies, have devised special measures for farmers who grow Bt crops. Farmers must plant a moat or "refuge" of conventional crops near their engineered crops. The idea is to prevent two resistant bugs from mating. The few insects that emerge from Bt fields resistant to the insecticide would mate with their nonresistant neighbors living on conventional crops nearby; the result could be offspring susceptible to Bt. The theory is that if growers follow requirements, it will take longer for insects to develop resistance.

It was difficult initially to convince farmers who had struggled to keep European corn borers off their crops to let the insects live and eat part of their acreage to combat resistance. But a 2001 survey by major agricultural biotech companies found that almost 90 percent of U.S. farmers complied with the requirements.

Many ecologists believe that the most damaging environmental impact of biotech crops may be gene flow. Could transgenes that confer resistance to insects, disease, or harsh growing conditions give weeds a competitive advantage, allowing them to grow rampantly?

"Genes flow from crops to weeds all the time when pollen is transported by wind, bees, and other pollinators," says Allison Snow. "There's no doubt that transgenes will jump from engineered crops into nearby relatives." But since gene flow usually takes place only between closely related species, and since most major U.S. crops don't have close relatives growing nearby, it's extremely unlikely that gene flow will occur to create problem weeds.

Still, Snow says, "even a very low probability event could occur when you're talking about thousands of acres planted with food crops." And in developing countries, where staple crops are more frequently planted near wild relatives, the risk of transgenes escaping is higher. While no known superweeds have yet emerged, Snow thinks it may just be a matter of time.

Given the risks, many ecologists believe that industry should step up the extent and rigor of its testing and governments should strengthen their regulatory regimes to more fully address environmental effects. "Every transgenic organism brings with it a different set of potential risks and benefits," says Snow. "Each needs to be evaluated on a case-by-case basis. But right now only one percent of USDA biotech research money goes to risk assessment."

Q: Can biotech foods help feed the world?

A: There are obstacles to overcome.

"Eight hundred million people on this planet are malnourished," says Channapatna Prakash, a native of India and an agricultural scientist at the Center for Plant Biotechnology Research at Tuskegee University, "and the number continues to grow."

Genetic engineering can help address the urgent problems of food shortage and hunger, say Prakash and many other scientists. It can increase crop yields, offer crop varieties that resist pests and disease, and provide ways to grow crops on land that would otherwise not support farming because of drought conditions, depleted soils, or soils plagued by excess salt or high levels of aluminum and iron. "This technology is extremely versatile," Prakash explains, "and it's easy for farmers to use because it's built into the seed. The farmers just plant the seeds, and the seeds bring new features in the plants."

Some critics of genetic engineering argue that the solution to hunger and malnutrition lies in redistributing existing food supplies. Others believe that the ownership by big multinational companies of key biotechnology methods and genetic information is crippling public-sector efforts to use this technology to address the needs of subsistence farmers. The large companies that dominate the industry, critics also note, are not devoting significant resources to developing seed technology for subsistence farmers because the investment offers minimal returns. And by patenting key methods and materials, these companies are stifling the free exchange of seeds and techniques vital to public agricultural research programs, which are already under severe financial constraints. All of this bodes ill, say critics, for farmers in the developing world.

Prakash agrees that there's enough food in the world. "But redistribution is just not going to happen," he says. "The protest against biotech on political grounds is a straw man for a larger frustration with globalization, a fear of the power of large multinational corporations. People say that this technology is just

earning profit for big companies. This is true to some extent, but the knowledge that companies have developed in the production of profitable crops can easily be transferred and applied to help developing nations."

Biotechnology is no panacea for world hunger, says Prakash, "but it's a vital tool in a toolbox, one that includes soil and water conservation, pest management, and other methods of sustainable agriculture, as well as new technologies."

The debate over the use of biotechnology in developing countries recently went from simmer to boil about rice, which is eaten by three billion people and grown on hundreds of millions of small farms.

"White rice," explains Dean DellaPenna, "is low in protein. It has very little iron, and virtually no vitamin A." However, in 1999 a team of scientists led by Ingo Potrykus, of the Swiss Federal Institute of Technology, and Peter Beyer, of the University of Freiburg, Germany, announced a new breakthrough: They had introduced into rice plants two daffodil genes and one bacterial gene that enable the rice to produce in its grains beta-carotene, a building block of vitamin A. According to the World Health Organization, between 100 million and 140 million children in the world suffer from vitamin A deficiency, some 500,000 go blind every year because of that deficiency, and half of those children die within a year of losing their sight. "Golden rice," so named for the yellow color furnished by the betacarotene, was hailed by some as a potential solution to the suffering and illness caused by vitamin A deficiency.

Skeptics consider golden rice little more than a public relations ploy by the biotechnology industry, which they say exaggerated its benefits. "Golden rice alone won't greatly diminish vitamin A deficiency," says Marion Nestle. "Beta-carotene, which is already widely available in fruit and vegetables, isn't converted to vitamin A when people are malnourished. Golden rice does not contain much beta-carotene, and whether it will improve vitamin A levels remains to be seen."

Potrykus and Beyer are now developing new versions of the rice that may be more effective in delivering beta-carotene for the body to convert to vitamin A. Their plan is to put the improved rices free of charge into the hands of poor farmers. According to Beyer, golden rice is still at least four years away from distribution. It could take much longer if opposing groups delay plans for field trials and safety studies.

Q: What next?

A: Proceed with caution.

Whether biotech foods will deliver on their promise of eliminating world hunger and bettering the lives of all remains to be seen. Their potential is enormous, yet they carry risks—and we may pay for accidents or errors in judgment in ways we cannot yet imagine. But the biggest mistake of all would be to blindly reject or endorse this new technology. If we analyze carefully how, where, and why we introduce genetically altered products, and if we test them thoroughly and judge

The Mechanisms of Genetics

them wisely, we can weigh their risks against their
benefits to those who need them most.

Reprinted with permission from *National Geographic.*

*How do you build a better fish? You start by
understanding what makes it a fish. In other
words, you delve into its DNA. Scientists at the
ARS [Agricultural Research Service] National
Center for Cool and Cold Water Aquaculture are
trying to learn about the rainbow trout—to find
out which genes help it to grow faster or to make
it more impervious to disease.*

*The scientists start by mapping the trout's
genes. Then they analyze the gene maps to
identify which ones lead to the most favorable
traits. What they learn about the trout's genetic
makeup will help them build stronger, more
disease-resistant fish to help both fish producers
and consumers. —SW*

"Improving Trout Through
Genetics Research"
by Sharon Durham
Agricultural Research, June 1, 2003

The ARS National Center for Cool and Cold Water
Aquaculture has been busy since its start-up in

August 2001. The tank/aquarium part of this new facility in Leetown, West Virginia, now holds 145 families of rainbow trout (*Oncorhynchus mykiss*). "These fish are lending their DNA for genetic analysis, and some are being grown at other research locations to determine how they perform under varying production conditions," says center director William K. Hershberger.

The center's research priorities include fish genetics and breeding, aquatic animal health, nutrition, production system development, and environmental compatibility. Initial research focuses on rainbow trout and other salmonids, but later research could include species such as striped bass, walleye, and yellow perch.

Fish and Chips

The first generation of breeder fish, formed by crossbreeding among two commercially used strains, is complete, says Hershberger. There are now 2,500 young fish from the first set of crosses at the center. They weigh an average of almost 2 pounds, and each has a computer chip embedded for individual identification.

Siblings of the breeder fish were shipped to other locations so their performance could be evaluated under different conditions. Some are being raised at the University of Idaho's Hagerman Fish Culture Experiment Station as part of the cooperative research program. Beyond evaluating growth and other performance traits in a different set of environmental conditions, the Idaho laboratory will also test the fish on different diets. The goal is to develop feeds that have more sustainable ingredients that are used more efficiently and allow the optimum expression of desired traits, such as rapid growth. (See article below.)

Other fish from the same family are being raised in a program with West Virginia University to evaluate their performance in small production unit conditions.

The center includes a 20,000-square-foot aquarium building with the latest in water-treatment and recirculation technology, much of which was developed from research conducted at the Conservation Fund's Freshwater Institute in Shepherdstown, West Virginia—another cooperator in the center's program.

The DNA Trail

Rainbow trout is one of the major U.S. fish crops. But there has not been much use of genetically based technologies to improve production efficiency in this species. ARS researchers are working hard to glean information from rainbow trout DNA that will be used to find out which fish grow faster, are more resistant to disease, or tolerate stress better. The first order of business is to identify fish that exhibit the desired traits based on family history. For instance, tracking the growth rates of fish can show which are the fastest growers. After individuals are identified with the desired traits, it has to be determined that these traits are indeed passed from parents to offspring. This is accomplished by using designed crosses and statistical analyses. Only after it has been confirmed can DNA analysis begin.

Molecular biologist Caird E. Rexroad III is working on a genetic map of *O. mykiss* that will assist in development of improved strains of the fish for aquaculture. To produce a genetic map, researchers collect blood or tissue samples from trout family members in which a certain trait is prevalent. Using various laboratory techniques, scientists isolate DNA from these samples and examine it for the unique patterns of base pairs seen only in family members having the trait.

Before researchers identify the gene responsible for a desired trait, like disease resistance, DNA markers can tell them roughly where the gene is on the chromosome. This is possible because of a genetic process known as recombination. As eggs or sperm develop within a trout's body, the chromosomes within those cells exchange—or recombine—genetic material. If a particular gene is close to a DNA marker, the gene and marker will likely stay together during the recombination process and pass on together from parent to offspring. If each family member with a particular trait also inherits a particular DNA marker, there is a high probability the gene for that trait lies near the marker.

The more DNA markers on a genetic map, the more likely it is that one will be closely linked to the desired trait gene—and the easier it will be for researchers to locate that gene.

"We are using microsatellite markers, which are repetitive stretches of DNA, to create the rainbow trout genetic map," says Rexroad. "This type of marker is easy to use with automated laboratory equipment so that researchers can rapidly map a trait in a large number of family members."

Rexroad and his colleagues have extracted DNA from each of the 145 families of trout and are adding 500 microsatellite markers they have produced to the genetic map. Rexroad hopes to eventually have 1,000 to 1,500 markers on the map to lay the groundwork for the next phase: functional genomics. Knowing where genes are on the chromosomes is good, but knowing their functions is essential to determining which fish possess specific desirable traits. "In the next year or so, we will be conducting DNA analyses that we hope will determine how these genes function," says Rexroad.

Lending a Helping Hand

In the fishery business, getting fish to marketable size quickly and efficiently makes a big difference in fish producers' financial successes. When finished, this trout map will be used to identify areas on the genome that affect production traits. The objective of the program is to develop a fish that benefits fish producers and consumers. The center is working with the University of Connecticut's Biotechnology Center in

Storrs, Connecticut, to find genes that enhance growth rate, increase disease resistance, and improve stress response. It may then be possible to produce transgenic rainbow trout that carry the genes for these qualities and then establish those transgenic founder lines for evaluation of performance.

"By the time this project is finished, our fish will be the most documented crosses of rainbow trout ever," says Hershberger.

Courtesy of the U.S. Department of Agriculture.

Web Sites

Due to the changing nature of Internet links, the Rosen Publishing Group, Inc., has developed an online list of Web sites related to the subject of this book. This site is updated regularly. Please use this link to access the list:

http://www.rosenlinks.com/cdfb/mege

For Further Reading

Butterfield, Moira. *Genetics: Present Knowledge—Future Trends*. Mankato, MN: Smart Apple Media, 2004.

Caporale, Lynn Helena. *Darwin in the Genome: Molecular Strategies in Biological Evolution*. New York, NY: McGraw Hill/Contemporary Books, 2002.

Hartwell, Leland, et al. *Genetics: From Genes to Genomes*. Boston, MA: McGraw Hill Science, Engineering, Math, 2003.

Jobling, Mark A., et al. *Human Evolutionary Genetics: Origins, Peoples & Disease*. New York, NY: Garland Science/Taylor & Francis Group, 2003.

Leroi, Armand Marie. *Mutants: On Genetic Variety and the Human Body*. New York, NY: Viking Books, 2003.

Ridley, Matt. *Genome: The Autobiography of a Species in 23 Chapters*. New York, NY: HarperCollins Publishers, 2000.

Rieder, Conly L. *Methods in Cell Biology: Mitosis and Meiosis*. San Diego, CA: Academic Press, 1999.

Watson, James D., and Andrew Berry. *DNA: The Secret of Life*. New York, NY: Alfred A. Knopf, 2004.

Wells, Spencer. *The Journey of Man: A Genetic Odyssey*. Princeton, NJ: Princeton University Press, 2003.

Bibliography

Ackerman, Jennifer. "Food: How Altered?" *National Geographic*, May 1, 2002, pp. 32–50.

BBC News. "Europe's 10 Founding Fathers." November 10, 2000. Retrieved August 3, 2004 (http://news.bbc.co.uk/1/hi/sci/tech/1015670.stm).

Beardsley, Tim. "A Clone in Sheep's Clothing." ScientificAmerican.com, March 3, 1997. Retrieved August 3, 2004 (http://www.sciam.com/article.cfm?articleID = 0009B07D-BD40-1C59-B882809EC588ED9F).

Boyce, Nell. "Triumph of the Helix." *U.S. News & World Report*, February 24, 2003, p. 38.

Caporale, Lynn Helena. "Foresight in Genome Evolution." *American Scientist*, May–June 2003, pp. 234–241.

"Chromosomes." Retrieved August 4, 2004 (http://users.rcn.com/jkimball.ma.ultranet/BiologyPages/C/Chromosomes.html).

Davies, Kevin. *Cracking the Genome: Inside the Race to Unlock Human DNA*. Baltimore, MD: Johns Hopkins University Press, 2002.

Durham, Sharon. "Improving Trout Through Genetics Research." *Agricultural Research*, June 1, 2003, pp. 4–7.

Dye, Lee. "Bringing Back the Tiger." ABCNews.com, July 8, 2004. Retrieved August 3, 2004 (http://more.abcnews.go.com/sections/scitech/dyehard/tasmanian_cloning_dyehard_040708.html).

Elliott, Ruan, and Teng Jin Ong. "Science, Medicine, and the Future: Nutritional Genomics." *British Medical Journal*, Vol. 324, June 15, 2002, pp. 1438–1442.

Gardiner, R. M. "The Human Genome Project: The Next Decade." *Archives of Disease in Childhood*, June 1, 2002, pp. 389–391.

Gibbs, Nancy. "The Secret of Life: Cracking the DNA Code Has Changed How We Live, Heal, Eat and Imagine the Future." *Time*, February 17, 2003, pp. 42–45.

"Goodbye Dolly . . . and Friends?" *The Lancet*, Vol. 361, March 1, 2003, p. 711.

Graff, James. "Living in the Past. Genetic Research Is Uncovering Signs That Our Ancestors Aren't What We Thought They Were—and That Most Europeans May Be Cousins." *Time International*, April 30, 2001, pp. 52ff.

Haseltine, William A. "Regenerative Medicine." *Brookings Review*, January 1, 2003, pp. 38–43.

Henderson, Mark. "Crick, the Genius Who Unravelled DNA." *Times of London*, July 30, 2004.

Human Genome Project Information. "Gene Therapy." Retrieved August 4, 2004 (http://www.ornl.gov/sci/techresources/Human_Genome/medicine/genetherapy.shtml).

Human Genome Project Information. "International Consortium Completes Human Genome Project." April 14, 2003. Retrieved August 4, 2004 (http://www.ornl.gov/sci/techresources/Human_Genome/project/50yr/press4_2003.shtml).

Human Genome Project Information. "SNP Fact Sheet." Retrieved August 4, 2004 (http://www.ornl.gov/sci/techresources/Human_Genome/faq/snps.shtml).

Jegalian, Karin, and Bruce T. Lahn. "Why the Y Is So Weird." *Scientific American*, February 1, 2001, pp. 56–61.

Kandel, Eric R. "Thomas Hunt Morgan at Columbia University." *Columbia Magazine*. Retrieved August 4, 2004. (http://www.columbia.edu/cu/alumni/Magazine/Morgan/morgan.html).

Lemonick, Michael. "Feb. 28, 1953: Eureka: The Double Helix." *Time*, March 31, 2003, p. A30.

Lewis, Edward B. "Thomas Hunt Morgan and His Legacy." Nobel e-Museum. Retrieved August 4, 2004 (http://www.nobel.se/medicine/articles/lewis).

McCall, Becky. "New Light Shed on Chimp Genome." BBC News, April 5, 2004. Retrieved August 3, 2004 (http://news.bbc.co.uk/1/hi/sci/tech/3594937.stm).

McClusky, Kevin. "Beyond Jurassic Park: Real Science with Ancient DNA." *Plant Health Progress*, October 19, 2000, p. 1094.

Mestel, Rosie. "Francis Crick—1916-2004; Renowned DNA Scientist Saw Life As It Is." *Los Angeles Times*, July 30, 2004, A1, p. 26.

Mlot, Christine. "Centromeres: A Journey to the Center of the Chromosome." *Science*, Vol. 290, December 15, 2000, pp. 2057–2059.

"Mouse Genome Sequenced." *Scientific American*, December 5, 2002. Retrieved August 4, 2004 (http://www.sciam.com/article.cfm?articleID = 00031D22-6C7C-1DEE-A838809EC588F2D7).

National Institutes of Health. "The Mouse Genome and the Measure of Man." National Human Genome Institute Press Release, December 2002. Retrieved August 4, 2004 (http://www.genome.gov/ page.cfm?pageID = 10005831).

Nijhout, Frederik H. "The Importance of Context in Genetics." *American Scientist*, Vol. 91, September 1, 2003, pp. 416–423.

Pacchioli, David. "Prisoners of Mendel." Penn State Online Research. September 2001. Retrieved August 3, 2004 (http://www.rps.psu.edu/ 0109/mendel.html).

Pennisi, Elizabeth. "Closing In on the Centromere." *Science*, Vol. 294, October 5, 2001, pp. 30–31.

Pennisi, Elizabeth. "DNA's Cast of Thousands." *Science*, Vol. 300, April 11, 2003, pp. 282–285.

Perry, Michael. "Extinct Tasmanian Tiger One Step Closer to Cloning." Reuters, May 29, 2002. Retrieved August 3, 2004 (http://www.enn.com/ news/wire-stories/2002/05/05292002/ reu_47364.asp).

Radford, Tim. "Metaphors and Dreams: The Paradox of the DNA Revolution Is That It Shows Us a Shining Future Without Telling Us How to Get

There." *The Scientist*, Vol. 17, Issue 1, January 13, 2003, pp. 24–26.

Rao, Giridhar. "Bioinformatics—New Horizons, New Hopes." *Drug Discovery & Development*, Vol. 7, July 1, 2004, pp. 18ff.

Rennie, John. "Celebrating the Genetic Jubilee: A Conversation with James D. Watson." *Scientific American*, April 1, 2003, p. 66.

"Rice Centromere, Supposedly Quiet Genetic Domain, Surprises." University of Wisconsin-Madison Press Release, January 13, 2004. Retrieved August 4, 2004 (http://www.sciencedaily.com/releases/2004/01/040111212949.htm).

Russo, Eugene. "Chimp Genome Released." *The Scientist*, December 12, 2003. Retrieved August 3, 2004 (http://www.biomedcentral.com/news/20031212/07).

"Sex Chromosomes." Retrieved August 4, 2004 (http://users.rcn.com/jkimball.ma.ultranet/BiologyPages/S/SexChromosomes.html).

Shute, Nancy. "The Human Factor." *U.S. News & World Report*, January 20, 2003, pp. 62–63.

Snedden, Robert, and Andrew Solway. *Cell Division and Genetics*. Chicago, IL: Heinemann Library, 2002.

"SNP Fact Sheet." Human Genome Project Information. Retrieved August 4, 2004 (http://www.ornl.gov/sci/techresources/Human_Genome/faq/snps.shtml).

Steinberg, Douglas. "Illuminating Behaviors." *The Scientist*, June 2, 2003, p. 18.

Travis, John. "Happy Anniversary: Fifty Years After Watson and Crick's Insight, Scientists Continue to Take a Close Look at DNA's Double Helix." *Science News*, Vol. 163, April 19, 2003, pp. 248–249.

University of Texas. "Bioinformatics." Retrieved August 4, 2004 (http://biotech.icmb.utexas.edu/pages/bioinfo.html).

Vangelova, Luba. "True or False? Extinction Is Forever." *Smithsonian*, June 1, 2003, p. 22.

"We Are What We Eat." *The Economist*, September 6, 2003, p. 28.

Index

A

Ackerman, Jennifer, 171
additivity hypothesis, explanation of, 56
Advanced Cell Technology (ACT), 29, 30
Agricultural Research Service National Center for Cool and Cold Water Aquaculture, 188–193
Archer, Mike, 26, 27, 28, 31

B

Bargmann, Cornelia I., 124–125
Baur, Erwin, 51, 53
behavior models, 119–126
Beyer, Peter, 186, 187
bioinformatics, 127–138, 166
biophobia, 99
Blair, Tony, 92
Brenner, Sydney, 119, 120
Brown, Bob, 30
Burns, James, 58, 59
Bush administration, 158

C

Cantor, Charles, 141
Caporale, Lynn Helena, 32–33
Carew, Thomas J., 120, 121
Carroll, Sean, 54

Cavalli-Sforza, Luca, 13, 15
Celera Genomics, 128, 131, 133
centromere, 79–80, 80–88
Charlesworth, Brian, 83
chimpanzee genome, compared to human, 12, 20, 24
chromosome duplication, 79
Clinton, Bill, 92, 101
cloning, 26, 27–31, 157
Colgan, Don, 29
common disease-common variant hypothesis, 117
Compaq Computer Corp., 131, 132, 133
complex traits/inheritance, 48, 49–66, 105, 106, 112, 115–117

 definition of, 50
conserved synteny, 115
Copenhaver, Greg, 83
Corning, 132
Crawley, Jacqueline N., 125, 126
Crick, Francis, 5–7, 9, 89–90, 91, 96
cross-species cloning, 29

D

Darwin, Charles, 9, 32, 33, 35, 98, 100
Dawe, Kelly, 82
Dayhoff, Margaret Oakley, 128

de Bono, Mario, 124–125
DellaPenna, Dean, 173, 177, 178, 186
Devlin, Bob, 173
Dickinson, W. Joe, 33
DNA
  discovery of structure, 5–6, 7, 89, 92
  DNA model's impact on science and health care, 90–96
  duplication from extinct animals, 23, 27–31
DNA Data Bank of Japan, 131
Dolly, 26, 28, 157
dominance, 50, 51, 57, 58, 59, 60
Double Twist, 128
Dubnau, Josh, 123
Dugatkin, Lee, 31

E
Enard, Wolfgang, 25
European Molecular Biology Laboratory, 131

F
Firestone, Karen, 29

G
Gamble, Clive, 19
Gardiner, R. M., 104–105
GenBank, 131, 144
gene flow, 17, 181, 183
gene therapy, 92–93, 102, 147, 151
genetic anthropology/heritage, 10, 11–20
genetic engineering
  of food/crops, 171, 172–188
  federal regulation of, 178, 180, 184

genetic malleability, 123
genetic plasticity, 122
genetic research on trout, 188–193
genomics, 93, 111, 112, 130, 136, 140, 148, 166, 192
Gibbs, Nancy, 89, 90
Gilbert, Dennis, 140, 141–142, 144–145
Gwynne, Peter, 139

H
Hall, Jeffrey C., 122, 123, 126
Haseltine, William A., 147
Heilig, Markus, 125
Heisenberg, Martin, 122
Hellmich, Rick, 182
Hershberger, William K., 189, 193
heterozygotes, definition of, 58
Hitachi, 131
Hofreiter, Michael, 23–24
homozygotes, definition of, 58
Human Genome Project, 7, 9, 69, 92, 96, 104–105, 105–118, 127, 129, 134, 136, 141, 149, 150
Human Genome Sciences, 147, 150, 151

I
IBM, 131, 132, 133
Incyte Corp., 128, 131, 132
Institute for Evolutionary Anthropology, 22
International Human Genome Sequencing Consortium, 7

J
Jegalian, Karin, 67–68, 76

K

Kacser, Henrik, 58, 59
Kandel, Eric R., 119, 120
Kaput, Jim, 169
Karpen, Gary, 85
Keith, Kevin C., 87
Klein, Richard, 22
Krauss, Ronald, 167–168
Krings, Matthias, 22

L

Lahn, Bruce T., 67–68, 72
Lanza, Robert, 30
Lewis, Ian, 30
Lim, Hwa, 128
linkage disequilibrium (LD),
    114, 116

M

Malyj, Wasyl, 165
McCombie, W. Richard, 83
meiosis, 71, 72, 79, 81, 82,
    85, 88, 114
Mendel, Gregor, 9, 48, 49, 50,
    54, 57, 118
methylation, 25
Microsoft, 132
minichromosomes, 82,
    87, 88
mitosis, 79
Monsanto, 177
Morgan, Thomas Hunt,
    118–119, 120, 122
Motorola Inc., 131, 132, 133
mutation
  definition of, 32
  random vs. strategic,
    33–48
Myriad Genetics Inc., 131

N

National Center for
    Biotechnology
    Information, 131, 144
National Human Genome
    Research Institute, 96
National Institutes of Health,
    144, 164
natural selection, 32–33, 33–48
Neanderthals, 16, 22, 24
Nestle, 169
Nestle, Marion, 180, 187
Nijhout, Frederik H., 48, 49
nonlinearity, 57, 58, 60, 64, 65
NutraGenomics, 169
nutritional genomics, 163,
    163–170

O

oncogenes, 55
Oracle, 131, 132, 133

P

Paabo, Svante, 20–21, 21–25
Page, David C., 67, 72, 76
Perlegen, 169
pharmacogenomics, 130, 140,
    142, 163, 165
phenotypic plasticity, 65
polymerase chain reaction
    (PCR), 20, 23, 29, 39
Potrykus, Ingo, 186, 187
Prakash, Channapatna, 184,
    185–186
Preuss, Daphne, 80–83, 85,
    86, 87, 88
Protein Information Resource
    International Protein
    Sequence Database, 132

R

Radford, Tim, 96
Rankin, Catherine H., 124
Rao, Giridhar, 127
reaction norm, 65
recombination, 71–79, 81, 83,
    85, 114, 148, 149, 161, 191
regenerative medicine,
    146–147, 147–162
Renfrew, Colin, 13, 18, 19
Rexroad, Caird E., III,
    191, 192
Richards, Martin, 10, 14
Rodriguez, Raymond, 168
Rudnicki, Michael, 55

S

Sachs, Eric, 177
Sandia National Laboratory, 131
Sanger, Frederick, 107
Sciona, 169
Seger, Jon, 33
Semino, Ornella, 10, 13–14
Serre, David, 24
sex chromosomes, evolution
    of, 67–68, 68–79
Silicon Graphics (SGI),
    132, 133
single nucleotide polymor-
    phisms (SNPs), 105, 106,
    113–114, 116–117,
    139–140, 140–146, 164
Snow, Allison, 181, 183, 184
spindle fibers, 79
StarLink, 179
Steinberg, Douglas, 119
stem cells, 153–155
  embryonic, 155–159

Stoneking, Mark, 16
Sun Microsystems Inc.,
    131, 132
SWISS-PROT, 132
Sykes, Bryan, 15, 17

T

Taylor, Steve L., 179
tetrad analysis, 83–84
thylacine (Tasmanian tiger),
    attempt to clone, 26,
    27–31
Trans Ova Genetics, 29
Tully, Tim, 123

U

Unilever, 169

V

Venter, Craig, 164

W

Wallace, Alfred Russel,
    33, 35
Watson, James, 5–7, 9, 89–90,
    91, 92, 96, 101
Wilmut, Ian, 26
Wilson, Allan, 23
Witkin, Evelyn, 43

Y

Yap, Greg, 140, 142,
    145, 146
Yin, Jerry C. P., 122–123

Z

Zoological Society of San
    Diego, 29
Zvelebil, Marek, 17

About the Editor

Stephanie Watson is executive editor of Mount Sinai's *Focus on Healthy Aging* newsletter. She is also a writer specializing in consumer health and science. She has written and contributed to more than a dozen works, including *Science and Its Times*, *World of Genetics*, *Science in Dispute*, and *The Endocrine System*. Ms. Watson lives and works in Atlanta, Georgia.

Photo Credits

Front Cover: (Top, left inset) © Inmagine.com; (bottom left) © Pixtal/Superstock; (background) © Royalty Free/Corbis; (lower right inset) © Alfred Pasieka/Photo Researchers Inc. Back Cover: (bottom inset) © Inmagine.com; (top) © Royalty Free/Corbis.

Designer: Geri Fletcher
Series Editor: Kathy Kuhtz Campbell